Just The Ticket!

A Comedy

John Waterhouse

Samuel French – London
New York – Sydney – Toronto – Hollywood

FOR AMATEUR PRODUCTION ENQUIRIES

UNITED KINGDOM AND WORLD EXCLUDING NORTH AMERICA

plays@samuelfrench.co.uk

020 7255 4302/01

Each title is subject to availability from Samuel French, depending upon country of performance.

JUST THE TICKET!

CHARACTERS

ETHEL LOVELOCK
MRS CARD (GRAN)
RUBY LOVELOCK
HARRY LOVELOCK
GERALD RUMBELOW
MR TRAVERS

The action of the play takes place in the Lovelocks' living room.

ACT I Scene 1   About 10.30 a.m.

        Scene 2   The same evening.

ACT II Scene 1   A morning a few days later.

        Scene 2   The following week on the eve of the wedding
                     about 11 p.m.

JUST THE TICKET! *

ACT I

Scene 1

The scene is the Lovelocks' living room. There is a door D.R. to the kitchen.
Above it a casement window. L.C. back wall there is a door which leads
into the hall. Off L. is the front door and stairs which lead to the bedrooms.
Next to the door is a built in cupboard. In the corner, shelves, and below
that more shelves. Downstage is a fireplace.

The furniture and furnishings are old and shabby. R.C. there is a dining
table with three chairs set around it. Beneath the, window a bookcase. There
is a sideboard set up against the R. back wall. GRAN's armchair is set above
fireplace. Below the fire is a low table on which stands the television.
There are cases of stuffed birds everywhere. The room is cluttered with them.
When the curtain rises it is about 10.30 in the morning. GRAN is discovered
in her armchair dunking ginger nuts in her large mug of tea. ETHEL
LOVELOCK sits L. of table stirring her tea absently. During a pause GRAN
makes rather disgusting sucking noises as she pops the biscuits into her mouth.

GRAN   He was at it again last night

---

*N.B. Paragraph 3 on page ii of this Acting Edition regarding photocopying and
video-recording should be carefully read.

ETHEL	(disturbed from her thoughts) I'm sorry, mother, what did you say?
GRAN	I said he was at it again last night.
ETHEL	Who was?
GRAN	Harry. I heard him tinkling up the stairs.
ETHEL	I know. He'd been to practice.
GRAN	If he knew what a fool he looked done up like he gets himself, he'd never do it.
ETHEL	He knows. He's seen himself in the mirror hundreds of times and it makes no difference.
GRAN	I'll tell you, if he was my husband I wouldn't have it. The least he could do is take them bells off when he comes in, then perhaps some of us could get a decent night's rest.
ETHEL	Why don't you tell him?
GRAN	I'm going to. I'm going to, don't you worry. I've had about enough of his jingling around in the middle of the night as I can stand. Of all the normal, respectable chaps who were grovelling at your feet when you were young, why you had to go and pick on him I'll never understand.
ETHEL	Don't let's go into all that again, please mother.
GRAN	And his bloomin' birds. If Peter Scott were to walk in through that door now – he'd go straight into mourning. It's like living in an aviary. Do you ever get the feeling they're watching you?
ETHEL	Now you're being silly. How can they? They're dead.
GRAN	I don't care. I do. I can feel their tiny eyes boring into me. (She shudders.) It's horrible. That husband of yours has some very nasty habits.
ETHEL	They're not habits, mother, they're hobbies.
GRAN	Call them what you like, but I still don't think they're right. He's never considered other people's feelings. They don't matter to him. He's selfish. He's the most self-centred man I've ever come across – are there any more ginger nuts?

ETHEL   (looking in the tin on the table)   There's only one left, I'm afraid.

GRAN   See what I mean? I'm even being denied me ginger nuts –

ETHEL   Of course you're –

GRAN   I don't ask for much in this life – just the odd, occasional ginger biscuit when I fancy one.

ETHEL   I'm so busy trying to economise I forgot to put them down on my shopping –

GRAN   I bet he put you up to it.

ETHEL   No he didn't. It's just that we've all got to make a few sacrifices until after the wedding. You want our Ruby to have a decent send off, don't you?

GRAN   What sacrifices is he making?

ETHEL   Well, er –

GRAN   None, that's how many. He still brings home his stuffed birds. He still goes out practising every week – and where does he practise?

ETHEL   You know as well as I do. Above the –

GRAN   – Swan and Sugarloaf. You don't honestly believe he and his fellow cranks stop above all night practising when there's all that boozing going on underneath them? If you believe that, Ethel, you'll believe anything. You've got to put your foot down, my girl. If we've got to make sacrifices then it's only fair that he should be made to go without as well.

ETHEL   Maybe you're right. Maybe I have been too lenient on him.

GRAN   Lenient! You've been put on. I've told you so all along but you wouldn't listen. No one can accuse me of not making life difficult for him. Heaven knows I've gone out of my way – is there any more tea left in the pot?

ETHEL   I'll have a look.   (She takes the pot across to GRAN and tops up her mug.)

GRAN   I think it's high time your Harry was brought up short. He's

	had his own way in this house for far too long. Why don't we show him who the real boss is, eh? I never left your poor father in any doubt right up to the time he died.
ETHEL	Before I was born.
GRAN	Yes, and a week after we were married. It was a week he never forgot.
	(RUBY LOVELOCK enters carrying a list.)
RUBY	Don't say he still hasn't come?
ETHEL	Who're you expecting?
RUBY	Gerald. We're supposed to be going through this guest list together. If I strike out any more names we might as well scrub the reception.
ETHEL	There's no need for that. Your dad only wants you to cut it down to within reason. When Frisby's told him it would cost fifteen shillings a head - he got that guillotined look.
RUBY	We're not still having it there, are we?
ETHEL	As far as I know.
RUBY	But we can't, not after dad wrote asking if they'd make a reduction if we took our own sandwiches.
ETHEL	It was only an enquiry.
RUBY	Why does he always have to go and spoil everything?
GRAN	Because he's mean and selfish, that's why.
RUBY	I thought a girl's wedding day was supposed to be the happiest day of her life.
GRAN	Don't you believe it. That's nothing but propaganda put about by men.
ETHEL	(going to RUBY)　　It is, luv. And yours will be, I promise you, in spite of the fact we're a bit short of cash -
GRAN	And your father can't stand the sight of the groom.
ETHEL	Mother! Really!
GRAN	It's the truth.
RUBY	(upset)　　Is it, mother?

ETHEL	(awkwardly) Well, er - no, not exactly -
RUBY	I know he's never said much to him, but I never knew he disliked him.
ETHEL	He doesn't. It's just that he finds him a difficult lad to get to know.
RUBY	(surprised) Gerald? Difficult? He's dead simple.
ETHEL	I'm sure he is - no, I don't mean that - I think your dad feels that they've got nothing in common.
GRAN	Which is a lot in the boy's favour.
RUBY	It's a marvellous time to find out, I must say, just as they're about to become related.
	(The front door is heard slamming off. HARRY LOVELOCK dashes into the room gasping for breath. His traffic warden uniform is somewhat dishevelled. He slams the room door and leans heavily against it. All the women look startled.)
GRAN	What the - !
ETHEL	Harry!
RUBY	Dad!
HARRY	Quick! Hide me!
ETHEL	What's happened?
HARRY	Never mind the questions, woman - hide me.
GRAN	Has he gone mad, Ethel?
HARRY	(snapping at her) No, I haven't. (To ETHEL.) If anyone knocks at that door - don't answer it.
ETHEL	Why ever not?
HARRY	Because I say so, that's why.
ETHEL	I wish I knew what all this was about.
GRAN	I don't like it. He's gone a funny colour.
HARRY	You'd have a funny colour if you'd been chased all the way from the city centre.

GRAN	He's done something, Ethel.
HARRY	(with meaning) I'll be doing something else in a minute. (Puffing.) It's no good. I'll have to sit down.
RUBY	You say you were chased, dad?
HARRY	Yes.
ETHEL	Who by?
HARRY	An aggrieved motorist.
GRAN	Serves you right.
HARRY	(turning on her) You mind your own business.
GRAN	(protesting) Are you going to let him talk to me like that?
HARRY	I don't have to get permission.
ETHEL	(to HARRY) There's no need to take it out on mother.
HARRY	Well, give her a ginger nut, only shut her up.
GRAN	There's only one left and I'm saving that for me tea.
HARRY	(wearily to ETHEL) Oh my godfathers! We're not in the middle of another ginger nut crisis, are we?
ETHEL	We won't go into that now.
RUBY	No, dad, tell us what happened.
HARRY	I was only doing my duty. I was coming up Porter Street when I caught this woman –
GRAN	I thought there'd be a woman mixed up in it somewhere.
HARRY	(keeping control of his temper) I caught her feeding a meter which had gone into the excess period. She didn't see me. I got me notebook out ready, patted her on the shoulder and said, 'Excuse me, Madam', and she turned round.
RUBY	Well?
HARRY	It were a long haired fella.
ETHEL) RUBY)	Oh, no!

HARRY   I was all ready to throw meself under an oncoming bus only
               he grabbed hold of me. Motorists don't reckon us much at
               the best of times, but when you pat one on the back and
               call him 'madam' they can turn very nasty.

ETHEL   And this one did?

HARRY   You're not joking! One look at his face told me all I
               wanted to know. I broke free and I ran. I don't want to
               boast, but I wouldn't mind betting I'm the fastest traffic
               warden north of Potters Bar.

ETHEL   Where were the police when all this was going on?

HARRY   Out catching criminals I shouldn't wonder. They leave
               homicidal motorists to us blokes.

               (There is a loud knock at the front door.)

               (in a frantic whisper)   It's her - him.

RUBY   Shall I go and see?

HARRY   (panicking)   You stay where you are.

RUBY   It might be Gerald.

HARRY   I don't care if it's the Fairy Snow Man - nobody opens that
               door.

               (There is more knocking at the front door.)

               If we stay quiet he might go away.

RUBY   If it is Gerald he'll be furious.

HARRY   A workout on that knocker'll do him good - help build up
               his muscles.

RUBY   You don't like him, do you?

HARRY   Who told you that?

RUBY   Gran.

HARRY   The old Kenwood mixer herself.   (To GRAN.)
               Have you been dropping me in it again?

GRAN   I only repeated what you said.

HARRY   You should take something for the repeating you do - try
               powdered glass.

RUBY	Well, do you, or don't you?
HARRY	Do I or don't I what?
RUBY	Like him?
HARRY	It's not a question of liking or disliking. I just don't think he's very healthy that's all. You've brought him home about five hundred times in the last six months -
RUBY	That's an exaggeration.
HARRY	It seems like it. He always seems to be here and he's either had a cold, got a cold or is about to get a cold.
ETHEL	He can't help that, poor lad.
RUBY	Of course he can't.
HARRY	I never said he could. But it's not very nice, is it? I mean you can hear him long before you see him. (He gives a loud sniff.) He's got more suction than our Hoover. If he could beat and sweep he'd have it made.
RUBY	Oh, dad! How can you!
ETHEL	You should be ashamed of yourself.
	(There is more knocking at the front door.)
HARRY	Quite frankly I don't think he'll get through the wedding service. When it comes to the part when he's asked, 'Wilt thou, Gerald Franklin Rumbelow, take this woman to be thy lawful wedded wife?' he won't know whether to sneeze, sniff or blow his nose.
	(RUBY starts to cry.)
ETHEL	Delightful!
HARRY	It's a fact. Mind you he should be all right for a few 'bless you's' from the vicar.
GRAN	Sacrilege now!
HARRY	But supposing he does get through it - with the help of his inhaler - and you settle down and have a family. What're the kids going to be like if they all take after him? (He gives a series of loud sniffs.) It'd be worse than living next door to an aerodrome. I wouldn't fancy it if it

was me.

RUBY   (petulantly)   Well, I'm not you and I do.

(There is more vigorous knocking on the knocker.)

And what's more I'm going to see if that's him at the door.
(She turns to exit.)

HARRY   (jumping to his feet)   No, no don't, please.

RUBY   You can't stop me.   (She flounces out.)

HARRY   (quickly crossing up to door and shouting after her)   If
it's a tall chap with long wavy hair - you'd better slam it
sharpish or I'll not be around to give you away.
(There is a slight pause. He crouches down in front of the
table. Nervously.)   This is worse than Russian
roulette.

GRAN   (contemptuously)   Call yourself a man?

HARRY   (snapping back)   No, do you?

(Offstage there is a sneeze followed by a loud sniff.)

(Getting to his feet obviously relieved.)   By hell! I
never thought I'd be glad to hear that.

(RUBY enters followed by GERALD RUMBELOW. GERALD
is a puny looking youth about the same age as RUBY. He
wears thick-lensed spectacles, has an appalling cold, and
an inflamed nose.)

GERALD   (complaining bitterly between sniffs)   What was the
big idea keeping me hanging about outside like that?

RUBY   I'm sorry, it was all a bit of a misunderstanding.

GERALD   I might've caught pneumonia.

HARRY   You'll never catch pneumonia, son - you haven't got the
strength to hold it.

RUBY   Dad thought you might've been someone else.

HARRY   You didn't happen to see a tall, long wavy-haired chap
with green trousers, pink shirt and open-toed sandals on
your travels, did you, Gerald?

GERALD   (amazed)   No, why? Are you looking for one?

HARRY	(aside to RUBY) Tell him to wipe his nose and I'll thump him.
ETHEL	(coming in quickly) How are you today, Gerald?
GERALD	I was all right until I got here, but all that knocking's taken it out of me.
ETHEL	Sit down a minute.
GERALD	Thanks. (He breathes heavily as he moves to sit down.) I'll be glad when you get a bell fitted. Hello Mrs Card. I didn't see you sitting there. I've brought something for you.
GRAN	(pleased) For me?
GERALD	(fishing about in his pockets) When I can find them. Your favourites. (He pulls a dirty crumpled bag from his pocket.) Ginger nuts.
GRAN	That's very kind of you, Gerald. You really shouldn't've bothered.
	(GERALD puts his hand in the bag and it comes straight out the bottom.)
HARRY	He hasn't from the look of things.
GERALD	Would you believe it! The bag's got a hole in! Never mind, they'll be in my pocket. You don't mind loose biscuits, do you? (He removes a grubby handkerchief and hands GRAN fistfuls of biscuits.)
	(ETHEL takes the tin from the table and hands it to GRAN who puts them in. HARRY watches the operation with distaste.)
GRAN	It's nice to know that there are still a few thoughtful people left in the world.
HARRY	If you'd take my advice you'd dunk those in hot Dettol.
GRAN	You keep your nose out of it.
HARRY	You want to tell him that, not me.
	(GERALD contorts his face as if he is about to sneeze.)
	Take cover!

GERALD   (the sneeze doesn't come)   It's funny, whenever I
                come here I always feel I want to sneeze.

HARRY   I've got just the cure for that – don't come.

ETHEL   He's only joking, Gerald, you know Mr Lovelock.

GERALD   It's the birds what do it. The feathers get up me nose.
                (He takes an inhaler from his pocket and holds it to one
                nostril as they all look on.)

HARRY   Here we go!

                (GERALD breathes in deeply.)

                Five, four, three, two, one – blast off! Hold on to it
                tight, son, or it might shoot out of the top of your head.

RUBY   (appealing to ETHEL)   Oh, mam, does he have to stay
                here making his rude remarks?

ETHEL   Harry, isn't it time you went back on duty?

HARRY   I'm not leaving this house until I'm sure that blond bomb-
                shell's not lurking in some alley waiting to bounce me.

RUBY   Then keep quiet. I want to go through the guest list with
                Gerald.

HARRY   (anxiously)   Keep it short, won't you, luv? Remember
                it's costing fifteen bob a head.

RUBY   (sarcastically)   Is thirty shillings going to be too much
                for you? Because up to now there's only going to be him
                and me there.

HARRY   No, no, that's reasonable. I just don't want you to go and
                do anything silly – like inviting your grandma.

GRAN   I heard that.

HARRY   You were meant to.

GERALD   I've been thinking.

HARRY   You should use that inhaler more often.

RUBY   What about?

GERALD   Do you think we're doing the right thing?

ETHEL   How do you mean, 'the right thing'?

GERALD	Getting married.
RUBY	(anxiously) You're not getting cold feet, are you?
GERALD	It's not that, only -
ETHEL	You've gone too far to back out now.
HARRY	(indignantly) He'd better not have.
	(ETHEL gives HARRY a look.)
GERALD	I don't want to back out. But I don't think we can afford to get married now that I've been made redundant and my dad's on National Assistance. I'll have to sell my rabbits to put a down payment on the ring.
HARRY	What if your rabbits die?
GERALD	Well, I could always sell the hutches.
HARRY	You're quite right, son, it's no good. We'll postpone it for twenty years or so.
ETHEL	We'll do no such thing. There's more to life than money.
HARRY	There is?
ETHEL	What about 'love'?
HARRY	Love's all right until the end of the month when the bills come in. You can't send them back with a few kisses at the bottom.
ETHEL	That's right. You throw cold water on everything. (To GERALD.) Have you thought about selling your car?
GERALD	I can't even give it away.
HARRY	You won't. They've introduced the combustion engine since that was built.
ETHEL	There must be something. Don't worry about it. I mean, you won't need a lot to start with. After all, you'll be living here with us.
HARRY	Yes. (Suddenly realising what's been said.) They'll what?
ETHEL	They'll be living here with us after they're married.

HARRY	Who said so?
ETHEL	It's all been arranged.
HARRY	(annoyed)　　Not by me it hasn't. Now, look here, Ethel –
GERALD	If we're going to live here those birds will have to go. I'm allergic to feathers, they get up –
ETHEL	Yes, well, we can talk about that later.
HARRY	No we bloody can't. Ethel –
ETHEL	(ignoring him)　　Look, Ruby luv, why don't you take Gerald into the other room and talk things over. I think your dad wants to say something and there's quite a lot your gran and me want to say to your dad.
RUBY	All right, mam, but don't let him bully you.
HARRY	Well, of all the –
ETHEL	(firmly)　　Those days are over.
RUBY	(hauling GERALD out of his chair)　　Come on useless.
GERALD	(as he is being dragged up to the door)　　Where're we going?
RUBY	Into the other room.
GERALD	(alarmed)　　Oh no! I'm not in the mood for –
RUBY	To make plans, stupid.
.GERALD	Oh!　　(His face suddenly contorts into a build up for a sneeze. He gives an enormous sneeze causing the picture over the fireplace to fall.)
	(RUBY drags GERALD out.)
HARRY	One of these days he'll have a ruddy ceiling down.
	(While ETHEL is replacing the fallen picture HARRY takes out an aerosol spray and commences to spray the room, especially the area where GERALD was sitting.)
ETHEL	What're you doing now?
HARRY	(continuing to spray)　　Fighting a one man war against his bugs. This is germ warfare.

B

ETHEL   With a fly spray?

HARRY   Why not? It'll bring down those that can fly and those
             that can't we'll stamp on.

             (ETHEL looks on as he crosses to GRAN's biscuit tin, picks
             it up, opens the lid and sprays the inside.)

GRAN   Put that down!

HARRY   I'm only decontaminating them.

GRAN   (snatching the tin from him)   You keep your hands off
             my things - cheeky beggar!

HARRY   (stops spraying. Pleased with himself)   I bet that's
             thrown them into confusion.

ETHEL   (snatching the spray from him)   There are times when I
             have my doubts about you.

HARRY   There's one doubt you can replace with a certainty - young
             Germicidal Gerald's not living under this roof while I'm
             here.

ETHEL   Is that a fact?

HARRY   It is. If they want to get married they can find a place of
             their own.

ETHEL   Where? Tell me that, where?

HARRY   Well, they could try the isolation hospital for a start.

ETHEL   For goodness sake, Harry, be sensible.

GRAN   You're asking a lot.   (She takes a nibble at one of her
             biscuits.)   You've ruined these biscuits.

HARRY   And they can take her with them.

GRAN   (making to rise)   That's it! I'll not stop down here to
             be insulted -

HARRY   I'll come up to your room.

ETHEL   You stay where you are, mother, ignore him. You were
             right. I never realised before just how selfish, self-
             centred and uncouth he really is. This has been a
             revelation to me. What sort of man is it who would set
             out to ruin his only daughter's chance of happiness? Deny

	her and her intended a roof over their heads? Cling to his creature comforts, waste money bringing home stuffed blessed birds and –
GRAN	Go out every night – practising.
ETHEL	If the Folk Festival Club means more to you than your own flesh and blood, then I suggest you go and live at the Swan and Sugarloaf.
GRAN	You can tinkle up and down their stairs and see how they like it.
ETHEL	Because we've had enough, Harry, more than enough. There's got to be some changes. Mother and me've been talking it over.
HARRY	I got the impression you might've done. If she's had anything to do with it it won't be so much of a change as a reign of terror.
ETHEL	That really depends on you. If you're prepared to co-operate we can all live together harmoniously. If you're not – I'm leaving –
HARRY	You wouldn't!
ETHEL	I would you know. I'll walk straight out.
HARRY	You can't mean it.
ETHEL	I mean every word of it, Harry.
GRAN	And I'd go with her.
HARRY	You make it very tempting. (To ETHEL.) What would I have to do?
GRAN	For a start –
HARRY	I wasn't talking to you.
ETHEL	For a start you spend no more money bringing home your feathered friends.
HARRY	No more birds?
ETHEL	No.
HARRY	But, Ethel, I've collected 'em all me life. Do you realise I've got one of the finest collections of tits in the country?

ETHEL	I don't care. You can either have them or me - please yourself.
HARRY	You're being unreasonable.
ETHEL	(firmly) Either them or me.
HARRY	(giving in) All right then. I won't buy any more. Is that all?
ETHEL	No. You finish with your Folk Festival nonsense.
HARRY	No, no, I won't do that. I refuse. I won't give up the Club. You don't honestly want me to give it up, do you?
	(GRAN sits there nodding. HARRY catches her.)
	What're you nodding for? I suppose that was your idea? (To ETHEL.) Let me go on with the Club, Ethel, please. I'm the Founder Member.
ETHEL	They can find somebody else because they're losing you. You've made a spectacle of yourself long enough.
HARRY	But it's our twentieth anniversary next week. They're making me a presentation. I'm not supposed to know -
ETHEL	You never will, because you'll not be there.
HARRY	We bring a lot of enjoyment to a lot of people.
GRAN	Not to me you don't with all your tinkling up and down stairs.
HARRY	(angrily) I've got a right to tinkle in my own house if I want to.
GRAN	Not when it keeps decent people awake all night.
HARRY	If you took a bottle of aspirins before you went to bed you'd never hear me.
GRAN	Did you hear what he said to me, Ethel?
HARRY	Do you want me to repeat it, Ethel?
ETHEL	No, I don't. And that's another thing. From now on you'll stop being rude to mother.
HARRY	Stop being rude to her? It's impossible.
ETHEL	In that case, there's nothing more to be said. Come on,

mother.

(GRAN again makes to rise.)

HARRY   No, wait a minute. Don't let's do anything hasty. I'll try not to be rude to her. It's a lot to ask, but I'll try.

ETHEL   You make sure you do.

HARRY   But she'll have to lay off me. She'll have to stop needling me. It's the ginger nuts what do it. She stuffs herself all day and gets overheated then takes it out on me when I come home.

ETHEL   I'm sure that's not true. Anyway you must make allowances.

HARRY   All right.

(HARRY and GRAN glare at each other.)

ETHEL   Good. Well, now we've got all that sorted out and we know how things stand, perhaps we can start making plans.

HARRY   Plans?

ETHEL   For our Ruby and Gerald. They'll live here.

HARRY   But –

ETHEL   (deliberately)   You would like them to live here, wouldn't you, Harry?

HARRY   Yes, yes, of course. But you heard what Gerald said – he's allergic to feathers. They get up his –   (He looks at all the birds round the room.)

ETHEL   I've thought about that. They can go up in the loft.

HARRY   He won't like it up there.

ETHEL   The birds, fathead.

HARRY   Oh.   (Horrified.)   My birds! Up – ?   (He points up.)   They'll get the moth up there.

ETHEL   They'll get the dustbin if they stay down here – so it's up to you.

HARRY   Hell fire! I should never've come back. I should've stayed and let that long haired chap clobber me. It couldn't've been worse than this.

ETHEL	Don't go feeling sorry for yourself because you haven't heard it all yet.
HARRY	There's more?
ETHEL	Since you won't have anything to do in the evenings now you have no hobbies, I suggest you start looking for a part-time job. The extra money you make we'll put on one side for the two children. How does that strike you?
HARRY	Stone cold.
ETHEL	But you must admit it's a good idea.
HARRY	(sarcastically) It is, yes.
ETHEL	When will you start?
HARRY	I haven't said I would. There's one small point I'd like to get cleared up. While I'm floggin' myself to death fining motorists by day and looking for work by night - what will you and her royal highness the ginger nut queen be doing?
ETHEL	We'll be pulling our weight don't you worry.
HARRY	I'm glad to hear it.
ETHEL	Playing bingo.
HARRY	Bingo!
ETHEL	I'm told the jackpot can be anything up to two hundred pounds. That's what mother and me'll be aiming for. Any more questions?
HARRY	No, no, that's all I wanted to know. I didn't like the thought that you might be sitting around enjoying yourselves.
ETHEL	(crossing down to kitchen door) Would you mind coming and giving me a hand in the kitchen, mother? I'm sure Harry wants to be alone for a few minutes - he's got a lot to think over.
	(GRAN struggles to get out of her chair.)
	Don't just sit there, Harry, help her.
HARRY	She can - !

ETHEL

Harry!

(Reluctantly HARRY crosses and helps the old lady to her feet.)

GRAN

(smiling as she crosses to join ETHEL)　　He's getting that same look your father had just before he died.

(ETHEL and GRAN exit.)

HARRY

Silly old buzzard!　　(He looks round the room for something to vent his feelings on. He spots the biscuit tin, picks it up, opens the lid and tips the contents on to the floor, flings the biscuit tin across the room and proceeds to jump on the biscuits with devilish glee.)

(RUBY enters.)

RUBY

What're you doing, dad?

(HARRY stops dead and stands looking very foolish.)

Are you feeling all right?

HARRY

Yes, yes - I was - I was just trying to get rid of these crumbs. Ruby, could I have a word with you?

RUBY

Not now, dad.　　(She crosses to kitchen.)　　I'm just on my way to make Gerald a hot drink.

HARRY

But Ruby -

(RUBY goes out.)

I'm being ignored! My authority is being put in jeopardy! (He crosses up for his cap.)　　By hell! Somebody's going to suffer for this!　　(He pulls the cap firmly down on his head. Vehemently.)　　I wouldn't be a motorist today for all the nuts in Brazil!　　(He takes out his ticket book and pencil and lifts his eyes heavenwards.) Please let me catch just one, just one parked on a yellow line. Amen.

(Suddenly there is a loud sneeze offstage, followed immediately by a thunderous crash.)

I've been answered.

(GERALD enters looking terribly pathetic, covered from head to foot in ceiling white and chunks of plaster. At first HARRY stands rooted to the spot as if he had seen a ghost.)

GERALD   I'm sorry, Mr – Mr – I sneezed –   (He gives a loud sniff.)

HARRY   It's you? I thought you were a messenger from –   (He looks up.)   You! You – !

(GERALD's face contorts into a further sneeze.)

Oh no you don't, my lad!

(HARRY grabs hold of him and practically drags him out towards the front door. Too late. There is another sneeze followed by another thunderous crash. HARRY slowly comes back into the room. He too is covered in ceiling white. GERALD follows him.)

GERALD   (very apologetically)   I've got a very sensitive nose.

HARRY   (rolling up the sleeve of his jacket)   You won't have in a minute.

(He grabs GERALD by the lapels and is about to put one on him when the kitchen door opens and ETHEL, GRAN and RUBY come in.)

RUBY   Dad!

ETHEL   Harry!

(HARRY turns and gives them a foolish smile. Unclenches his fist, pats GERALD on the cheek and starts to brush him down.)

CURTAIN

Scene 2

The scene is the same about 6.30 in the evening.

When the curtain rises the first thing we notice is that all the stuffed birds have been removed. GRAN is having forty winks in her chair. ETHEL enters from the kitchen and starts to lay a single place at the table. She wears an apron over a smart dress. When she is satisfied that she has everything on the table, she looks across at GRAN and gives a warm smile and returns to the kitchen.

After a short pause the door opens slowly and HARRY's head appears as if to make sure the coast is clear. He shows surprise when he notices that the birds have flown and comes into the room and frantically looks round. He mutters something under his breath, looks murderously towards GRAN and goes out and re-enters immediately carrying a stuffed owl which stands about two feet high. He stands admiring it then presses a small switch on base and its eyes flash on and off. He smiles, shaking his head fascinated. Thinking he hears someone coming, he moves quickly up to the built-in cupboard, opens the door and places the owl on one of the shelves. Just as he is tiptoeing to hang up his cap and haversack –

GRAN   (eyes still closed)   What're you creeping about for?

HARRY   (nervously)   Who? Me? I – I – wasn't creeping.

GRAN   You were creeping. I know a creep when I hear one.

HARRY   (crossing down to her)   You were asleep. I didn't want to disturb you.

        (GRAN gives a grunt.)

        A sudden shock could kill you, you know. I must remember that.

GRAN   What was that?

HARRY   I've brought you these.   (He holds out an unopened packet of ginger nuts.)

GRAN   Why?

HARRY   I don't know. I suppose you could call it a sort of peace offering since we're going to be nice to each other.

GRAN   (taking the packet and examining it suspiciously) What've you done to them?

HARRY   (angrily)   I've not done anything to them, you silly

old –   (Trying to control his anger.)   I had an
accident with your others so I bought you some fresh ones.

GRAN   It's not like you.

HARRY   I know it's not – I wish I hadn't bothered now. They're
quite safe. Here, I'll show you if you like.   (He
snatches the packet from her, tears it open, takes out a
biscuit and crams it into his mouth.)

(ETHEL enters from kitchen carrying a plate of pilchards on
toast.)

ETHEL   (annoyed)   Oh, Harry! You're not eating before your
tea, surely?

HARRY   (with his mouth full)   No, I was just showing your
mother I wasn't trying to poison her. What's the use!

ETHEL   There's no point in me slaving over a hot stove if you're
going to stuff yourself with biscuits.

HARRY   It's no good! You can't win!   (He drops the packet of
biscuits in GRAN's lap.)   You'll have to chance it.
(He takes his ticket book from the haversack.)   I've
had a good haul today, Ethel. I've booked eight.

ETHEL   That's nothing to be proud of. Poor devils! How would
you like it if you were a motorist?

HARRY   I'm not. That's why I got the job. It's the 'have nots'
against the 'haves' and we're winning. I've discovered
today the secret of success. You offer up a prayer to
St Christopher, then hide in a doorway where you can't be
seen. It never fails.

ETHEL   I'm glad I don't have to live with your conscience, that's
all.

HARRY   It's not all one sided, you know. They try it on as well.
Like today. I'm not kiddin' you, there was a car parked
across a zebra crossing with a Guinness label for a licence.
A Guinness label! It was still on the bottle.   (He
looks down at his meal.)   Hello! What's this?

ETHEL   Pilchards in tomato sauce.

HARRY   That's a relief – it looked worse.

ETHEL   If you don't want it you know what you can do. I've been
             too busy all afternoon picking up fallen ceilings to fuss
             over food.

             (HARRY sits and stares at his plate.)

             When are they coming?

HARRY   I don't know. But whoever they are I hope there aren't
             many of them if this is all there is to eat.

ETHEL   The builders to fix the ceilings!

             (HARRY looks blank.)

             You did call in, I take it?

HARRY   No.

ETHEL   No?

HARRY   It doesn't seem worth it if Gerald's coming here to live.

ETHEL   How do you make that out?

HARRY   Given six months and a dose of flu' I reckon we'll need to
             rebuild.

ETHEL   That's just like you that is, always making excuses. If you
             won't see to it I will. I have to do everything around here.
             I take it you've noticed the birds have flown?

HARRY   I was going to ask you about them.

ETHEL   They've migrated to the loft.

HARRY   Then on your head be it, Ethel. I've got a fortune tied up
             in those birds.

ETHEL   If only you had, Harry, if only you had.

HARRY   It only needs a touch of damp in their stuffing and that's it –
             we'll be up to our knees in down.

ETHEL   Do you intend sitting and staring at that all night or are
             you going to get it eaten?

HARRY   (looking at the pilchards)   It's not a pretty sight, is it?
             Give it to the old cat.   (Turning to GRAN.)   It's
             all right, mother, I didn't mean you.

ETHEL   It won't eat things with sauce on.

HARRY	Only I'm expected to do that.
ETHEL	(leaning across him to get at the plate) Excuse me.
HARRY	What's the rush?
ETHEL	I'm in a hurry.
HARRY	That's a good enough reason. What for?
ETHEL	Mother and me are going to bingo.
HARRY	Tonight?
ETHEL	I wouldn't be tearing around like this if it was tomorrow, would I?
HARRY	What about me?
ETHEL	What about you?
HARRY	What am I supposed to do with myself?
ETHEL	(handing him a newspaper) Start looking down the situations vacant and see if you can find some night work.
HARRY	I can't see in the dark.
	(RUBY enters dressed in her outdoor clothes. She looks fed-up.)
ETHEL	(surprised) Hello, what're you doing here? When you went out this afternoon you said not to expect you home until late.
RUBY	He never showed up.
ETHEL	Gerald?
RUBY	We arranged to meet outside the Odeon at six – he never came.
ETHEL	He may have been held up somewhere.
HARRY	Or propped up somewhere.
RUBY	Do you think he's all right? He didn't look well when he left here this morning.
ETHEL	You're never at your best when you've had a couple of ceilings fall on you.
HARRY	(laughing) It's the first time I've ever seen him with

any colour.

RUBY   (angrily)   It's not funny. He might've been killed.
              Look, just because you don't like him there's no need to
              be always getting at him. He's terrified of you.

HARRY   Of me? I can't think why.

RUBY   Neither can I, but he is. I'll give you fair warning, dad,
              if you do or say anything to spoil our wedding I'll never
              speak to you again as long as I live.

ETHEL   You've got it all wrong, luv. He's not out to spoil
              anything. In fact he wants to help you, don't you, Harry?

HARRY   What?

ETHEL   You want to help them?   (To RUBY.)   He was just
              going through the evening paper as you came in to see if
              he could find some night work to get a few extra pounds
              together for you.

RUBY   (contrite)   Were you really, dad?

HARRY   Yes, yes, I've always thought the nights were too long.
              All that time wasted sleeping when I could be out making
              money.   (Glancing at the paper.)   Mind you,
              there doesn't seem to be much of a choice. It's a toss up
              whether I'm a brush and shovel man at the greyhound
              stadium or a hot dog vendor in an all night café.

ETHEL   There you are you see. You're fond of animals so either of
              those would suit you.   (To RUBY.)   He'll find
              something, I'll see to that.

RUBY   I'm sorry, dad, I blew my top.   (She gives him a peck
              on the cheek.)

HARRY   That's all right, luv.

ETHEL   (suddenly remembering)   Ruby! I've just remembered!
              (She picks up a parcel which stands about fifty inches high,
              wrapped in sacking.)   This came for you while you
              were out.

RUBY   (excited)   I wonder what it is?

ETHEL   A British Railways van –

HARRY	(nodding towards the parcel) Get away! That's never a British Railways van.
ETHEL	(looking hard at HARRY) - delivered it this afternoon.
HARRY	Oh.

(ETHEL and RUBY start to undo the string.)

RUBY	I wonder who it can be from?
ETHEL	We'll soon know. Isn't it exciting getting presents? I've been dying to open it ever since it arrived. Then like a ninny I have to go and forget it. Nobody sent us any presents when your dad and me got married.
GRAN	That's not true, Ethel. I did.
HARRY	You never sent it. You brought it with you when you came to stay.
RUBY	What did you give them, gran?
HARRY	(nodding towards GRAN) That chair.
GRAN	It's a very comfortable chair.
HARRY	So it ought to be. You had it made to measure. (To ETHEL.) Haven't you got it undone yet?
ETHEL	Very nearly.

(ETHEL and RUBY pull away the sacking and packing paper to reveal a naked pink cherubic figure with hands raised above its head supporting a bowl. There is a label about its neck. They all stand staring at it open mouthed. Pause.)

RUBY	What is it?
ETHEL	I don't know, but whatever it is, it's very rude.
GRAN	I can't see.
ETHEL	It's better you didn't, mother. It's not very respectable.
RUBY	What does that label say?
HARRY	(reading from label) 'Lot 41. Slightly imperfect'.
ETHEL	Indecent would be nearer the mark.

RUBY	Funny there's no card to say who it's from.
ETHEL	(to HARRY) Some of your friends send saucy postcards. You don't think it could be one of them?
RUBY	What am I going to do with it?
HARRY	If we knew what it was we'd tell you. (He removes the bowl and examines it.)
RUBY	I'll never get that in my bottom drawer.
HARRY	You'd have a hell of a job to get that in your wardrobe.
ETHEL	See if it'll go under your bed.
HARRY	Only remember it's there or you could have a nasty shock in the middle of the night coming face to - face with that.

(RUBY with ETHEL's assistance picks the statue up in her arms swathed in the sacking. It looks more like a babe in arms. HARRY hands her the bowl.)

If you need any help - shout down for your mother.

(There is a loud knock offstage.)

ETHEL	I'll go. (She exits.)
RUBY	It might be Gerald.

(There is a loud sniff off.)

HARRY	It couldn't be anybody else.

(GERALD comes striding into the room furiously. ETHEL follows him on looking bewildered. GERALD's face and hands are covered in oil. He carries a small slip of paper and crosses to HARRY.)

GERALD	(angrily) Mr - Mr - (Suddenly his face contorts into a sneeze.)
HARRY	Hold it a minute. (He rushes across to picture above the fireplace and holds it.) Ready when you are.

(GERALD gives an enormous sneeze. HARRY gives the ceiling an anxious look then lets go of the picture which drops.)

ETHEL	Now why should he do that? There are no birds in here now.

(HARRY shrugs innocently then glances quickly at the cupboard.)

GERALD   Mr Lovelock –

RUBY   Aren't you talking to me then? What've you been doing?

GERALD   (turning to face her. Pointing to the bundle in her arms) I might ask you the same. Whose is that?

RUBY   If you must know it's ours.

GERALD   (panic stricken)   Ours! You mean – ? It can't be!

RUBY   It was delivered this afternoon.

GERALD   This afternoon! But – you've never – we've never – oh dear!

RUBY   We don't even know what it is.

ETHEL   Except that it's very ugly and has no clothes on.

RUBY   I was just going to see if I could stick it under my bed.

GERALD   You can't do that!

RUBY   Have you got a better suggestion?

          (GERALD is too stunned to answer.)

          It's not living with us.

ETHEL   How about your mam? Perhaps she would like it?

GERALD   The shock'd kill her if she ever found out.

ETHEL   It's not as bad as all that.   (She takes the bowl from RUBY.)   This goes with it.

HARRY   (taking the bowl from ETHEL)   He holds it over his head like this.   (He strikes a similar pose to that of the cherub.)

GERALD   Have you all gone potty?

HARRY   I never thought of that.   (To ETHEL.)   You don't think it's a – ?

          (ETHEL shakes her head.)

          No, no, perhaps you're right.

GERALD — What's the matter with you all? Do you know what you're saying? That's our baby you're talking about. Your own flesh and blood and you want to stick it under beds - give it away -

RUBY — Baby?

ETHEL — Flesh and blood?

HARRY — It's happened! I knew it would sooner or later - all that sneezing's shaken his brains loose.

RUBY — (looking down at the bundle in her arms and realising GERALD's confusion) You've got it all wrong, Gerald. (She holds up the bundle.)

GERALD — (stepping forward like an anxious father) Mind you don't drop him!

RUBY — This isn't a baby, silly.

GERALD — It's not?

RUBY — No.

GERALD — Are you sure?

RUBY — It's a wedding present. You can see for yourself. (She pulls back the sacking.)

(They all laugh at GERALD.)

GERALD — (angry) That's right, go on, laugh at me. How was I supposed to know? Well, you know what you can do with it, don't you? You can send it back where it came from, because as far as I'm concerned the wedding's off.

RUBY — Off?

ETHEL — What're you saying, Gerald?

GERALD — (excited) I'm saying there's going to be no wedding, that's what I'm saying.

RUBY — But why? What's happened?

GERALD — You really want to know? Because of him. (He points accusingly at HARRY.) He doesn't like me. He never has. But this afternoon was the last straw. (He crosses to HARRY and hands him the piece of paper he's been

	holding in his hand.) Is that your signature on that parking ticket?
HARRY	(examining the ticket) Yes. Where did you find it?
GERALD	As if you didn't know. It was stuck on my car.
RUBY	Oh, no!
GERALD	Oh, yes!
ETHEL	Oh, dear! Which one of the eight were you?
GERALD	I was the one broke down on the zebra crossing.

(ETHEL looks at HARRY who winces.)

GERALD   I've been flat on my back under that car for over three hours and when I got out I found this stuck behind me (He sniffs.)   wiper. If he'd've troubled to bend down he could've given it to me in person, but not him, hit and run that's him. I'll tell you Ruby, as long as he's in that job you'll never marry a motorist.

HARRY	Now, listen to me –
GERALD	I don't have to. (He holds up ticket.) I've got it in writing. (He turns to go.)
ETHEL	There must've been some mistake. Mr Lovelock would never –
HARRY	That's enough, Ethel. When I need a spokesman I'll let you know. There's been no mistake. He committed an offence and got done and that's an end to it.
GERALD	It's victimisation! (He marches up to door.)
HARRY	And while you're about it get that licence changed – the bottle's expired.
GERALD	I've only got one thing to say to you and that's – (His face starts to crease and he sneezes.)
HARRY	And I've only got one thing to say to you – stop splashing our ruddy woodwork!

(GERALD storms out.)

RUBY	(in tears and shouting after him) Gerald! Don't go! Gerald! Gerald, wait for me! (To HARRY.)

How could you? How could you! (She dumps the
cherub into his arms and dashes out.)

(There is a menacing pause.)

ETHEL   (turning on HARRY)   Are you satisfied? Are you
feeling pleased with yourself?

HARRY   Look, Ethel, I was only carrying out my duty.

ETHEL   As a traffic warden maybe, but not as a father. I dread to
think what damage you've done now.

GRAN   He's selfish! Selfish to the core!

HARRY   If she says that once more I'm going to have to be very
rude to her.

ETHEL   (warning him)   Don't you dare. I don't want her
upset as well. I suppose you realise Ruby'll never forgive
you for what you've done?

HARRY   I didn't even know it was his car.

ETHEL   Would it've made any difference if you had?

HARRY   No.

ETHEL   Then what're you blathering about? The moment you put
that uniform on the world's your enemy. You get power
mad.

HARRY   I do what I'm paid to do.

ETHEL   You don't have to enjoy it. The way you dish out those
tickets anyone would think you worked on commission.

HARRY   He was on a zebra crossing.

ETHEL   I don't care if he was on an elephant's back - he was your
son-in-law to be. The question now is is he to be or not to
be?

(RUBY enters sobbing into her handkerchief.)

RUBY   (brokenly)   He's gone, mam.

ETHEL   (going to her and putting a comforting arm round her)
There, there, luv. I know how you feel, but it's not the
end of the world.

RUBY   He said he'd never come back.

ETHEL   He didn't mean it.

HARRY   (contritely)   Ruby, I'm –   (He steps forward and
              realises that he has the cherub. He hands it to GRAN.)
              Here, it's your turn.   (He crosses to RUBY.)   I'm
              sorry if I've –

RUBY   Don't talk to me. Don't ever talk to me again.

HARRY   (trying to explain)   I didn't know it was –

ETHEL   You heard what she said.

GRAN   Leave the girl alone.

HARRY   (protesting)   I was only doing my duty.

ETHEL   If you say that once more I'll scream.

HARRY   I'll pay his fine for him.

RUBY   That won't bring him back.

HARRY   He's not dead – only from the neck up. How would it be if
              I took a couple of ten hour cold tablets and went and had
              a long chat with him?

ETHEL   You'd do that?

RUBY   It's too late now.

ETHEL   He could try. He could explain and offer to pay his fine
              and talk to him man to man –

HARRY   I hadn't thought about going as far as that.

ETHEL   No, but you will, won't you?

HARRY   Yes, if you think it'll help.

ETHEL   It'd better for your sake. Well go on then if you're going –
              only get out of that Gestapo uniform first or you'll get his
              back up straight away.

HARRY   Shall I walk or go on my hands and knees?

ETHEL   How you get there is no concern of mine just so long as you
              go.   (To RUBY.)   Your gran and me are going to
              bingo at St Mary's Hall. Why don't you come with us?
              It'll help take your mind off things.

(HARRY removes the jacket of his uniform.)

RUBY   I'm not in the mood for bingo.

ETHEL   There's nothing to be gained moping about here. We can't
            do anything until the peace mission returns.   (She
            looks at HARRY.)

RUBY   All right then. You're sure you don't mind?

ETHEL   Of course not. If we're going we'd better start thinking
            about getting ready.   (She crosses to GRAN.)
            Come on, mother.   (She takes the cherub from her.
            To RUBY.)   You don't really want this cluttering up
            your bedroom, do you?

RUBY   No, not really.

ETHEL   Right, we'll stick it in this cupboard for now.

HARRY   (panic stricken)   No!

ETHEL   I beg your pardon?

HARRY   I said no.

ETHEL   What do you mean 'no'?

HARRY   You don't want to put it in there.

ETHEL   Have you got a better idea?

HARRY   No - yes - the - the - coal shed.

ETHEL   All right -

HARRY   (relieved)   Good.   (He goes to take it from her.)

ETHEL   - we'll put it in the coal shed tomorrow. It can go in the
            cupboard for now.

HARRY   No, no! I'll take it out. I don't mind.   (He attempts
            to take it from her.)

ETHEL   Tomorrow.

HARRY   Now.

            (They tug at the cherub.)

GRAN   Are we going out for bingo or stopping home for tug o' war?

ETHEL   I don't know what's got into him. Will you let go of it!

(She snatches the cherub out of his grasp.)   Are you hiding something in there you don't want me to see?

HARRY   No, no, of course I'm not –

ETHEL   Then it's going in.   (She flings the cupboard door wide open.)

(The owl's eyes flash on and off. HARRY stands cringing. ETHEL lets out a scream, steps back, drops the cherub and quickly shuts the door.)

GRAN   (clutching at her heart, terrified)   For mercy's sake! What's happening?

ETHEL   (nervously clasping HARRY)   Did you see it, Harry?

(HARRY nods.)

What do you think it is?

HARRY   I know what it is – it's a ruddy owl with a short circuit.

ETHEL   An owl?

HARRY   A long eared Asio Flammeus.

ETHEL   (incredulously)   Are you trying to tell me that you've brought another damned bird home after all what I – I don't believe it! You wouldn't be such a –   (She slowly opens the cupboard door. The owl's eyes continue to flash on and off.)   – you would!

HARRY   I couldn't resist it, Ethel. You don't find many with eyes that – it's a novelty –   (He takes it from cupboard.)

ETHEL   So, tonight's to be novelty night, is it? Right, here's another for you – we're leaving!

HARRY   (shaken)   Now, now –

ETHEL   Mother, go upstairs and start getting packed – you too, Ruby.

HARRY   You don't have to do that.

ETHEL   Don't I just. I told you. I warned you what'd happen if another bird came into this house. Well, it's happening right now.   (To RUBY and GRAN.)   Come along, don't let's hang around.

HARRY   I'll take it back.

ETHEL   Don't bother - you've bought it - play with it.

HARRY   (trying desperately to find the switch to stop the eyes from
               flashing on and off. He finds it but it doesn't work. To
               the owl)   Stop it you - !   (He puts his hand over
               its eyes.)   I'll take it straight back, now, this very
               moment. I'll knock the chap up -

ETHEL   It's no good, Harry. You're feather brained and incurable.
               We're going and nothing you can say or do will stop us.

               (The three women go out.)

HARRY   Ethel!   (He moves up to door and shouts after them.)
               Ethel! Don't leave me - please. I'll take it back. I'll
               burn it. I'll do anything you like with it only don't go -
               Ethel - Ethel - can you hear me?   (He turns viciously
               on the bird.)   It's all your fault! You and your
               flashing flippin' eyes!   (Angrily he grabs at the piece
               of wire between the bird's legs, pulls it free and throws it
               away. The eyes immediately stop lighting up.)
               Serves you right!   (He does a take on the bird as he
               spots something near the tail feathers. He pulls it free.
               It is a tightly rolled piece of paper. It turns out to be a
               five pound note.)   A bloomin' fiver!   (Holding it
               up to the owl.)   Have you got any more where that
               came from?   (His curiosity roused he examines the
               bird and discovers another and another. His excitement
               grows with each fresh find. After the fourth fiver he is
               unable to contain himself any longer.)   I've heard of
               a nest egg, but this is ridiculous!   (He takes a bread
               knife from the sideboard and lays the bird on its back to
               cut it open.)   You don't have to look like that. It
               won't hurt a bit.   (He takes a handkerchief from his
               pocket and places it over the bird's head. He picks up
               the knife and goes through the motions of making an
               incision. He then puts in his hand and removes bundle
               after bundle of notes. One time he pulls out a bag of
               coppers. Disgusted.)   How the hell did that get in
               there?   (He throws the bag on to the floor, then
               returns to the bird and produces more bundles of notes.
               When he is satisfied that there are no more he does a rough

count of the bundles. Counting.)   – thirteen, fourteen,
fifteen – fifteen hundred pounds! (He burst out
laughing.)   We're rich! We're loaded!   (He
rushes to the door and shouts upstairs.)   Ethel – we're
rich! Come down here, quick. Ma, Ruby, come and see
what I've found.   (He picks up bundles of notes in his
arms, hugs them to him and allows them to tumble on to
the table as he picks up the owl. To Owl.)   I'll see
you get the finest taxidermist in the country for this.
What stuffing would you prefer? Cotton wool? Nylon
wadding? Or sage and onion?   (He laughs and gives
the owl a couple of smacking kisses on its beak.)

(Just then ETHEL, GRAN and RUBY enter wearing their
outdoor clothes and carrying suitcases.)

GRAN   He's gone birdserk, Ethel!

HARRY   And so will you when you see what I've found. Look!
            (He holds up bundles of notes for them all to see.)

ETHEL   (putting down her case as if in a trance and crossing to
            HARRY. She takes a bundle from him and stares at it)
            Where did you get this?

HARRY   Not just that, luv, but all this an' all.   (He steps
            back from the table indicating the rest of the money.)

            (The three women gather round.)

RUBY   (appalled)   What've you done, dad?

GRAN   What indeed?

ETHEL   Where did you get it?

GRAN   I wouldn't mind betting he's been fiddlin' the parking
            meters.

HARRY   No you wouldn't, but you'd be wrong. If you must know
            I got it from a wealthy old bird.

RUBY   (shocked)   Not another woman?

GRAN   I wouldn't put it past him.

ETHEL   Just let me catch him!

HARRY   No, no, no.   (Holding up the owl.)   From him –

her - this.

ETHEL	You mean - ?
HARRY	Yes. Somebody's been using him as a piggy bank.
ETHEL	Piggy bank? But how? How did they get it in there?
HARRY	I suppose they used to stick it in - stick it up - no wonder its eyes lit up. Do you know how much there is here? Over fifteen hundred pounds.
ETHEL	(savouring it) Fifteen hundred pounds!
HARRY	(to GRAN) Or enough to keep you wallowing in ginger nuts until you're a hundred and forty.
RUBY	And it's all ours.
HARRY	(correcting her) And it's all mine.
ETHEL	What do you mean 'yours'?
HARRY	What I said. I mean - you won't be here, will you? You're all packed up to go. You're leaving me.
ETHEL	Oh, no, not now we're not. There's been a sudden change of plan. You don't think we're going to leave you with fifteen hundred pounds and however much more there might be up there. (She points up.)
HARRY	Up where?
ETHEL	In the loft. (To RUBY and GRAN.) You and gran get your things off, get a knife and get in that loft and see what you can find. Start on the ducks and the parrots.
	(RUBY and GRAN quickly collect knives from the sideboard and go out. There is a look of horror on HARRY's face.)
	(shouting after them) You can leave the swan to me!
HARRY	You mean you're going to - ? Ethel, you mustn't. You mustn't let them. (He rushes to the door.) Mother! Ruby! Come down!
ETHEL	(picking up the bread knife from table) You said yourself you'd got a fortune tied up in those birds.

HARRY   I know I did, but I didn't mean that –

ETHEL   We'll go and see, shall we? To think there might be a
               million pounds roosting over our heads this very moment
               just waiting to be plucked.   (She goes out with a look
               of dedication on her face.)

HARRY   (pleading)   Don't pluck please.   You'll find nothing.
               (He stands in the hall.)   The owl was a fluke. A
               million to – what am I saying?   (As he stands outside
               the door, feathers in all colours and sizes float down on
               him from above. He looks up pitifully.)   Spare me
               tits!   (He examines a feather which has just landed
               on him.)   Too late!   (He looks very unhappy.
               His face suddenly contorts and he gives an almighty
               sneeze. The picture over the fireplace drops and part of
               the ceiling above his head collapses. He stands looking
               powerless. He raises his arms and allows them to fall by
               his side.)   It's been one of those sort of days!

               CURTAIN

ACT II

Scene 1

A few days later.

The room appears to have been completely refurnished apart from GRAN's chair.

When the curtain rises ETHEL is discovered staggering about with a newly acquired tall rubber plant. She tries it on several pieces of furniture but is not happy with the result.

GRAN sits in her chair dunking biscuits in a new, highly decorated mug. There are six packets of unopened ginger biscuits stacked by her chair.

ETHEL	(still looking for a resting place for the plant) Now I've got the blessed thing I don't know where to put it.
GRAN	I've told you once. Try it in the hall.
ETHEL	No. We'll never see it stuck out there. I paid good money for this and I mean to get the benefit of it. (She sets it down on the dining table and stands back.) It's not right there, but it'll have to do.
GRAN	(looking at it with distaste) What's it supposed to be?
ETHEL	It's not supposed to be anything - it's a rubber plant. Harry says they grow them from elastic bands - I don't believe him.

(GRAN takes another biscuit from an opened packet on her lap.)

Do go easy on those biscuits, mother. It's your third packet since yesterday. |
GRAN	They're mine. I can do what I like with them.
ETHEL	Yes, I know, but -
GRAN	It's all I got out of that fifteen hundred pounds. No three piece suites, carpets, televisions, curtains, rubbery plants for me - just a dozen packets of ginger biscuits.
ETHEL	And the mug, don't forget the mug. It's very pretty.

Harry picked it himself.

GRAN   (looking at it)   I thought so. It's the sort of thing he
        would pick. Have you read what it says round the side?
        (Reading from the mug.)   'Sup it up don't sup it down
        case you topple in and drown' and it's cracked.

ETHEL   It never is.

GRAN   It's cracked, I tell you, right down one side. I bet he got
        it cheap.

ETHEL   Never mind, we can always change it for another. We
        shouldn't complain really, should we? We've got a lot to
        be thankful for. To think only a couple of days ago we
        were penny pinching and wondering what to do for the best
        and now look at us.   (She looks round the room.)
        I still can't quite believe it.

GRAN   (feeling the bottom of the mug)   It's leaking!

ETHEL   Mind you I feel bad about destroying poor Harry's birds.

GRAN   (feeling her lap)   I wondered where it was coming
        from −

ETHEL   It seems so pointless now. It's not as if we found anything.
        And the look on his face as we came down those stairs.
        He'd aged ten years.

GRAN   (examining her skirt)   This stain'll never come out.

ETHEL   These last couple of nights've been terrible. He's been
        having nightmares. Haven't you heard him calling out?

GRAN   Who's been calling out?

ETHEL   Harry. 'Where's my cock robin? Let go of my parrakeets!'
        He gave me a real fright last night. He jumped out of bed
        and ran across to the window flapping his arms screaming
        'I'm a yellow headed finch!'

GRAN   Nothing he does surprises me.

ETHEL   If I hadn't caught him when I did he'd've flown straight
        out. I don't mind telling you I'm worried. If he keeps it
        up I'll have to get him to an ornithologist.

        (There is a loud knock at the front door.)

I wonder who this could be?   (She exits. Voice off.)
Thank you.   (She re-enters very excited carrying a
large dress box.)   It's come!   (She puts the box
on the table and shouts upstairs.)   It's come, Ruby!
It's here!   (She moves quickly back to the table and
starts to untie the string.)

(RUBY rushes in excitedly, wearing a housecoat.)

RUBY   Where?   (She spots the box on the table and crosses to
it. Looking at the rubber plant.)   Oh, mam! That's
not stopping there, is it?

ETHEL   (annoyed)   It'll have to for now, there's nowhere else
for it.

RUBY   Can't it go in the hall?

GRAN   That's what I said, but no, she wants to sit and look at it.

RUBY   It's in the way.

ETHEL   (even more annoyed)   Oh, all right, all right.
(She picks it up.)   I wish I'd never bothered with it.
(She goes out.)

(RUBY takes the dress out of the box. It is her wedding
dress.)

RUBY   (holding it up in front of her for GRAN to see)   Oh,
look, gran. Isn't it beautiful?

GRAN   (grunts)   All I got was twelve packets of biscuits.

RUBY   And the mug, gran, don't forget the mug. It's very pretty.
Dad picked it himself.

GRAN   It's leaked all over me lap.

(ETHEL enters.)

ETHEL   It doesn't look right out there either.   (When she sees
RUBY with the dress she stops enraptured.)   Oh, Ruby!
Oh, Ruby, it's lovely!

RUBY   Do you like it?

ETHEL   (crossing to her)   Like it? I think it's the most
gorgeous thing I've ever seen in my life. Are you going to
try it on?

RUBY   What now?

ETHEL   (encouraging her)   Go on, luv, let's have a look at you.

RUBY   All right.   (She starts to take off her housecoat.)

ETHEL   (helping her)   I always wanted to get married in white. There's something so pure about white, don't you think?

RUBY   What were you married in?

ETHEL   A bottle green sweater and jodhpurs. Not that I wasn't pure, but I was still in the Land Army.

GRAN   She had to marry your dad in a hurry.

ETHEL   You don't have to say it like that.   (To RUBY.) He was due to be posted overseas so it was all a bit of a rush.

GRAN   It was a mistake.

ETHEL   It was very romantic at the time. His friends and mine formed an arch outside the church - pitch forks and bed pans - he was in the Medical Corps. And the things they tied to the wedding car.   (She laughs.)

GRAN   It was shameful!

ETHEL   They meant no harm.   (She zips up the back of RUBY's dress.)

            (RUBY puts the veil on and strikes a bridal pose.)

            (stepping back and admiring her)   You look a dream, Ruby.   (To GRAN.)   Doesn't she look a dream, mother? When Gerald sees you walking up the aisle - (She starts to sniff and takes out a hanky.)   I hope he realises what a treasure he's getting.   (She starts crying and takes hold of RUBY.)

RUBY   Don't cry, mam, it might shrink the veil.

ETHEL   (releasing her)   I'm sorry luv, all of a sudden I got a mental picture of it all. You and him standing there together - have you managed to persuade him to get a morning suit?

RUBY   It took some doing, but he promised to go in for a fitting

	this morning.
ETHEL	Good. Now, that only leaves your father.
RUBY	He must, unless he wants to be the odd man out.
ETHEL	He won't be the odd man out, don't you worry. He's just being stubborn.
GRAN	He'll dress up and make a fool of himself for his Folk Festival fandangoing but not for his daughter's -
ETHEL	(to GRAN) Don't you go and say anything to him or you'll put the kybosh on it straight away. Leave him to me. I've just got to get over his prejudice of not wanting to look like a penguin and we'll be all right.
HARRY	(voice off) Anybody at home?
ETHEL	(to GRAN) Remember what I said, mother - not a word. (Shouting.) We're in here!
HARRY	(voice off) What the - ! (He enters wearing his uniform and carrying the rubber plant.) What the hell's this doing stuck in the hall?
ETHEL	I put it there out of the way.
HARRY	I've got news for you. It wasn't out of the way.
ETHEL	(snatching it from him) Trust you! (She marches out with it.)
HARRY	(seeing RUBY) Hello! Is it all over? Did I get the dates wrong?
RUBY	No, dad -
HARRY	(obviously disappointed) Oh!
RUBY	I put it on to show mam and gran. Well, do you like it?
HARRY	(without enthusiasm) Yes, yes, it's very nice.
ETHEL	(as she enters) You might try and sound a bit more enthusiastic.
HARRY	You know my feelings about wedding dresses - they're like fireworks. Use 'em once and what've you got?
ETHEL	That's just like a man.

HARRY	And that's just like a woman. When you haven't got a reasonable argument that's what you always say. 'That's just like a man.'
ETHEL	(to RUBY) Don't take any notice of him, luv.
HARRY	And if that doesn't work you pretend he isn't there.
ETHEL	That's the sort of mood we're in, is it?
HARRY	I'm not in any sort of a mood.
ETHEL	Are they driving away too fast for you this morning?
HARRY	(cross) No they're not.
ETHEL	There's something the matter.
HARRY	Do you know how much of that fifteen hundred quid there is left?
ETHEL	I might've guessed! It's the money!
HARRY	Four hundred flippin' quid. Four hundred! I've just put six hundred and fifty pound deposit down on that bungalow for them.
RUBY	(excitedly) Oh, dad, you haven't!
HARRY	Oh, dad, I have!
RUBY	(going to him and hugging him) You're an angel!
HARRY	I won't be for much longer if your mother goes on clipping my wings as she has been.
ETHEL	Let's spend it while we've got it. You're a long time dead.
HARRY	Do you think we could put a bit on one side for the funeral? There's over three hundred quids worth of new stuff in this room for a start and that's not counting the old lady's mug. (To GRAN.) By the way, do you like it? I thought it was very pretty. I picked it myself.
GRAN	It's cracked.
HARRY	Then you'll always know it's yours, won't you?
GRAN	It's made a mess on me lap.
HARRY	What's made a mess on your lap?

GRAN

My tea.

HARRY

You shouldn't drink your tea out of your lap. What do you think I bought the mug for?

ETHEL

She's trying to tell you it leaks.

HARRY

They said it might. Never mind. Here.   (He takes a wad of notes from his pocket, peels one off and drops it in GRAN's lap.)   Go and buy yourself another one. Why stop at one?   (He peels off more notes and lets them flutter down into her lap.)   Buy seven. Have a mug a day. The neighbours'll be knocking themselves sick trying to keep up with us.   (To RUBY.)   Did they send a bill with that dress?

RUBY

I didn't look.

HARRY

You'd better then - while I've still got some loot left to pay for it.

RUBY

(searches the box and finds it)   I've got it.   (She looks at it and nervously hands it to HARRY.)

HARRY

(looks at it and his face drops)   Thirty five guineas!

ETHEL

(amazed)   Is that all?

HARRY

What do you mean, is that all?

ETHEL

They must've made a mistake.

HARRY

I hope you're right.

ETHEL

(taking the bill from him and examining it)   I thought as much. I knew it couldn't be right. They haven't included the two bridesmaids dresses.   (She hands him back the bill.)

HARRY

(stunned)   Bridesmaids dresses?

ETHEL

Yes, in pink taffeta. It shouldn't be more than another eighteen guineas.

HARRY

Eighteen guin - ! Couldn't we cut it down by half? One brides whatsit wearing her own clothes?

ETHEL

No, we couldn't, Harry. It'd spoil the whole look of the thing. Besides they're made. While I remember. You won't have to worry about the cars.

HARRY   That's a relief. I'll be able to transfer that worry to
          something else. What cars?

ETHEL   The wedding cars, silly.

HARRY   Wedding - ? I thought we were walking. The church is
          only a couple of hundred yards up the road.

RUBY   And how do we get to the reception afterwards?

HARRY   What's wrong with the bus?

ETHEL   Give over, Harry.

HARRY   There's a stop bang opposite on the other side of the road.
          A sixpenny fare right to the city centre.

ETHEL   The cars will be here at eleven thirty sharp.

HARRY   You'd better be ready. There's a yellow line outside this
          house. I don't want to have to be out there writing
          summonses while the bride's mother hunts for her gloves.

ETHEL   (shocked)   You wouldn't?

HARRY   (chuckling)   No. But it conjures up a funny picture,
          doesn't it? I don't want to appear unusually ignorant, but
          isn't the groom and his lot supposed to make some financial
          contribution to this little outing?

ETHEL   It's normal, yes, but -

HARRY   Gerald isn't, is that it?

ETHEL   No, that's not it. We can't expect them to put their hands
          in their pocket now they know we've had this windfall.

HARRY   Hells bells!

ETHEL   Which reminds me - bells.

HARRY   (grumbling)   You can't open your mouth in this house
          without you remembering something.

ETHEL   (to RUBY)   The vicar wants to know if you want a peal
          or a hymn.

HARRY   What's the difference?

ETHEL   About fifteen shillings.

HARRY   I shouldn't've asked.

ETHEL   (to RUBY)   I said I thought you'd want a hymn and you'd let him know which one when you've decided.

HARRY   Who's paying?

ETHEL   Who do you think?

HARRY   Right, I decide. You can tell him we'll have 'The Sower Went Forth Sowing'.

GRAN   The girl's getting married not gathering in the harvest.

HARRY   How do you know what she'll be doing?

ETHEL   (to HARRY)   That'll do.   (To RUBY.)   You and Gerald talk it over.

               (There is a knock at the front door.)

               (looking at her watch)   It'll be another wedding present I expect.

HARRY   If it's C.O.D. like the last one tell 'em to take it back.

               (ETHEL exits.)

               (to GRAN)   It's time your side of the family paid for their own presents.

ETHEL   (voice off. Surprised)   Hello, Gerald, luv! Come in. (She appears at the door.)   It's Gerald.   (Turning to Gerald who is still off.)   Mind the –

               (There is a loud china crash off.)

               Never mind, you couldn't help it.   (She comes into room.)

               (GERALD enters in full morning dress which is a shade too large for him all round. His top hat has dropped over his eyes and he can't see where he is going. He staggers about clutching the rubber plant by the stem with the roots trailing. Under his arm he carries a large brown paper parcel, in which is his suit.)

HARRY   (to ETHEL)   Isn't he going to find that a bit big for his buttonhole?

ETHEL   (taking the plant from GERALD)   For the first time I know what to do with it.   (She places it in the waste-paper basket.)

GERALD   (attempting to remove his topper)   Is Ruby here?

RUBY   Yes, I'm here, luv.

              (GERALD manages to get the topper above his eyes.)

ETHEL   (rushing to him frantically)   Oh, good heavens,
              Gerald. Don't look!   (She bangs his hat over his eyes
              again.)

              (GERALD staggers under the blow.)

HARRY   What's the matter with you, Ethel?

ETHEL   It's bad luck for him to see his bride in her wedding dress
              before –

HARRY   Well, he needn't think he's having the good luck of seeing
              her without it while I'm here. We don't want him getting
              all excited before he has to.

              (GERALD manages to raise his topper past his eyes again.)

ETHEL   It's too late, now, the damage has been done. I only
              hope it doesn't bode ill, that's all.

              (There is a pause as they all stare at GERALD. He grows
              more and more selfconscious and starts to fidget.)

GERALD   (giving a sniff and grinning foolishly)   I've done it!

HARRY   Yes, you look as if you might have.

GERALD   I mean, I've been and got myself fitted out. They
              suggested in the shop I come and show you, to see what
              you think. What do you think?

HARRY   It'd be unkind to tell you.   (To ETHEL.)   And
              you want me to look like that?

ETHEL   Yes, why not?

HARRY   (laughing)   I should say so!

ETHEL   (unconvinced)   I think he looks very smart. It just
              needs taking in here and there.

GERALD   It's already been taken in here and there. I'm one big
              tuck from top to – I can't sit down and be comfortable.

	(Appealing to RUBY.) Can't I wear me best suit, Rube?
RUBY	No.
ETHEL	Certainly not. There's nothing nicer than a man with tails.
HARRY	If we were meant to have tails we'd've grown 'em. If he turns up at the church like that, ten to one they'll never let him in.
ETHEL	(examining the suit) There must be something we can do to make it fit.
GERALD	They said I was between sizes.
HARRY	That's the story of your life. You're either between sizes or between jobs. (To ETHEL.) I'll tell you what Ethel. If you can make him look remotely presentable in that I'll go down to town first thing tomorrow and get myself togged out.
ETHEL	Is that a promise?
HARRY	It's more than a promise - it's a ruddy challenge.
ETHEL	Right - you're on!
HARRY	(to GERALD) I wouldn't be in your shoes now, son, for all the Steppes in Russia.
GERALD	(nervously) Why? What're they going to do?
HARRY	If they can't make that suit fit you - they'll make you fit the suit.
ETHEL	He's only pulling your leg.
HARRY	Somebody'll have to or else we'll never see his feet. (He lifts the leg of GERALD's trousers.) About four inches should do it.
ETHEL	You leave it to us.
HARRY	Right. I'd better get back on duty.
GERALD	Do you have to?
HARRY	(looking at his watch and taking out his book) They'll all be out there now, lulled into a sense of false security, Just waiting for the law to take its course. I'm not going

to disappoint them.   (To ETHEL.)   I'm patrolling
round here, luv, so I'll be in for dinner.   (He puts a
friendly hand on GERALD's shoulder.)   Be brave, lad.
Remember it's going to hurt you a damned sight more than
it is them.   (He turns and goes out.)

(There is a pause. GERALD stands rigid with fear.)

ETHEL   (walking round him sizing him up)   Where shall we
start?

GERALD   (sniffing nervously)   I'd rather you didn't bother.

ETHEL   But we must.

GERALD   I want to go home.

(ETHEL ignores him.)

Please can I go home?

ETHEL   No.

GERALD   I'm only here on appro.

ETHEL   Ruby, go and fetch my peg bag.

RUBY   Peg bag?

ETHEL   That's what I said.

(RUBY shrugs her shoulders and exits into the kitchen.)

GERALD   What're you going to do to me, Mrs Lovelock?

ETHEL   Not Mrs Lovelock, luv, you'll have to start calling me
mother.

GERALD   I might have to start calling for help. What're you going
to do to me?

(RUBY comes in with the peg bag.)

ETHEL   You'll see. I'll need your assistance, Ruby.   (She
takes the bag from RUBY and the parcel from GERALD.)
You won't want this.   (She puts the parcel on the
table.)   Now, stand up straight.

GERALD   (hurt)   I am standing up straight — it's the suit what's
at ease.

ETHEL   (businesslike)   We'll soon have that right.   (She removes his topper and gives it to GRAN.)   Mother, will you pack the inside rim with paper and make it smaller for him. We want him to be able to see what he's doing. (She returns to GERALD and takes a few pegs from the bag.)   I want you to watch me, Ruby, then do what I do on the other side of him.   (She finds the shoulder seam, makes a tuck in it and pegs it. She puts several pegs along the shoulder, the seam in the sleeve, etc.)

(When RUBY sees what her mother is doing she copies her, doing exactly the same. Ad. lib. dialogue.)

GERALD   (to RUBY. Crying out in pain)   Ouch! You've got some of me in there!

RUBY   (pegging away at speed)   Don't be such a baby!

GERALD   (as they continue to peg him)   I'm not happy about this.

ETHEL   You will be when we've finished with you.

GERALD   Now I know what a Christmas tree must feel like.

(Soon GERALD is festooned in pegs. Every seam in both coat and trousers is lined with pegs.)

ETHEL   (standing back to take a look)   It's looking better already. Turn round.

(GERALD turns full circle with difficulty.)

How does it feel?

GERALD   Sore.   (He wriggles uncomfortably, puts his hand behind his back, sucks in his breath, winces and produces a peg. Holding it up.)   Can you manage without that one? Only it brings tears to me eyes when I cough.

GRAN   (holding up hat)   See how that is.

(ETHEL takes the hat from her and puts it on GERALD's head. It perches.)

ETHEL   That won't do at all. It makes him look ridiculous.

(There is a knock at the front door.)

Now what? If it's not one thing it's another. I'll go. (She exits.)

GERALD   (looking miserable)   I'm not going to look like this on
            the day, am I?

RUBY   Of course not, silly. It's all got to be sewn.

GERALD   That's all right. I don't want everyone to know I got it off
            the peg.

            (ETHEL comes into the room followed by TRAVERS, a
            middle-aged man wearing a trench coat and carrying a
            trilby.)

ETHEL   (apologetically) ·   You'll have to excuse us. We're all
            at sixes and sevens this morning, I'm afraid.

TRAVERS   I'm the one who should apologise. I seem to have called
            at -   (He stops speaking on seeing GERALD.)

ETHEL   (smiling foolishly)   We're just making a few minor
            adjustments to him.   (Introducing RUBY.)   This is
            my daughter Ruby, Mr - Mr - ?

TRAVERS   Travers.

ETHEL   Mr Travers -

            (RUBY and TRAVERS shake hands.)

            And this   (introducing GERALD.)   is her husband-
            to-be, Gerald.

TRAVERS   Congratulations young man.

            (GERALD takes hold of the lapels of his coat and pulls
            them down sharply causing the pegs on his shoulders to
            spring off. He looks surprised. He then shakes hands
            with TRAVERS.)

ETHEL   And this is my mother.

            (TRAVERS turns to GRAN, clipping a peg on the index
            finger of his right hand as he does so.)

TRAVERS   (to GRAN)   How do you do?   (He holds out his
            hand, sees the peg, unclips it and hands it to GERALD.)
            It'd be a pity to spoil the set.

            (GERALD takes it from him and looks for somewhere to
            clip it.)

ETHEL	Mr Travers is making an enquiry.
TRAVERS	I really wanted to speak to your husband.
ETHEL	You've just missed him. But I'm sure we'll be of more use to you. We're used to these enquiries.
TRAVERS	Really?
ETHEL	Oh, yes. We have people like you round three or four times a week wanting to know what coffee we drink, the soap we use. You name it, they've been. Which one are you?
TRAVERS	Since you put it like that I suppose you could say I'm making an enquiry about money.
ETHEL	Money?
TRAVERS	Yes. (Looking round the room at the new furniture and furnishings.) You've been using quite a lot of it by the look of things.
ETHEL	You mean the suite?
TRAVERS	It looks new.
ETHEL	It is. It was only delivered yesterday. And this carpet, and the one in the bedroom, the TV set and the curtains and –
TRAVERS	A mug I believe?
ETHEL	That's right. How did you know about that?
TRAVERS	It's all part of my enquiry.
ETHEL	We've never had one like you before.
	(GRAN holds up the mug.)
TRAVERS	(crossing to GRAN and taking the mug from her) This is the mug, is it? Very pretty. (To ETHEL.) Your husband picked it himself.
ETHEL	Yes. (Puzzled.) You know a lot about us.
TRAVERS	Pity it's cracked. (Handing GRAN back the mug.) Still, things are never quite what they seem at first glance, are they, Mrs Lovelock?

ETHEL	(a little apprehensively) No, I suppose they're not. Would you like to sit down?
TRAVERS	I prefer to stand if you don't mind.
ETHEL	(uneasily) Oh. What is it you want to know exactly?
TRAVERS	Quite a lot, Mrs Lovelock, quite a lot. For instance (He puts his hand in his jacket pocket and produces a five pound note. He holds it up for all to see.) do you recognise this?
ETHEL	(relaxing) We've had this before, mother. It's one of those quizzes. (To TRAVERS.) What do we get if we guess right?
TRAVERS	That's not for me to say.
ETHEL	Oh, well, never mind, it'll come as a surprise. It's a five pound note.
TRAVERS	Correct.
ETHEL	Next question.
TRAVERS	Can you tell me the serial number?
ETHEL	You've got me there.
TRAVERS	(reading from note) C98405061.
ETHEL	Oh.
TRAVERS	Do you know where I got this from?
ETHEL	I haven't got the faintest idea.
TRAVERS	What if I told you it came from Randall's Furnishings?
ETHEL	But that's where we got the three piece suite and the carpets and –
TRAVERS	Precisely. It is one of the seventy your husband paid over to them.
ETHEL	Then what are you doing with it?
RUBY	There isn't anything wrong is there?
TRAVERS	That rather depends on how you came to be in possession of three hundred and fifty pounds of stolen notes.

ETHEL   Stolen!

RUBY   Oh no!

GRAN   I knew it! I knew it! I knew Harry was a crook the first
               time I set eyes on him.

GERALD   Does that mean the other eleven hundred and fifty he's got
               left was stolen an' all?

               (They all turn and look at GERALD, horrified.)

TRAVERS   My, my! We do seem to be in a bit of bother, don't we?

               (The front door is heard to slam. HARRY rushes in.)

HARRY   (as he enters)   I forgot to leave this -   (He has a
               piece of paper in his hand. He stops dead in his tracks on
               seeing all the solemn faces.)   Has somebody cracked
               a joke?   (He comes further into the room and sees
               GERALD.)   Oh, I see - the groom's pegged out.
               (He laughs and turns to TRAVERS.)   The groom's
               pegged -   (The laugh dies.)   Am I interrupting
               something?

TRAVERS   Mr Lovelock?

HARRY   That's right. Is that your car parked out front?

TRAVERS   Yes, why?

HARRY   I'll deal with you in a minute.   (He turns to GERALD.)
               I forgot to give you -

ETHEL   Harry -

HARRY   Just give me a second with sunshine here. I've got some
               explaining to do.

RUBY   You don't understand, dad -

HARRY   I do, but I've got me doubts if he will.   (To GERALD.)
               I want you to concentrate, Gerald. Are you concentrating?

               (GERALD nods.)

               (turning to TRAVERS)   It's not always easy to tell with
               him.   (To GERALD.)   I've put down the six
               hundred and fifty pounds deposit for the bungalow and
               arranged with the building society for a mortgage for you.

	Now, all you have to do –
RUBY	But, dad –
HARRY	Don't keep interrupting, luv, or I'll never get through to him. (To GERALD.) You see this form? All you have to do is answer the questions only be careful what you put. Like here, for instance (Reading.) where it says 'sex'. You don't have to go into details – just tell them what you are. (He looks at him for a moment.) On second thoughts it might be better if you went into details. And this one. (Reading.) 'Have you suffered from the following?' If you answer 'yes' to any of those they won't give you a brick never mind about a house. (Reading.) 'Present occupation?' 'Unemployed' isn't going to help you much. If I were you, I'd put 'under contract to the Ministry of Labour'. It's the same thing, but it sounds better. Have you got the idea?
GERALD	I think so.
HARRY	Then I'd get it filled in while you're still warm. (He gives GERALD the form and turns to TRAVERS. Using his official voice.) Now, sir, about your car.
	(Both HARRY and TRAVERS produce black books from their pockets simultaneously.)
ETHEL	(crossing to HARRY) Harry, you've got to listen to me.
HARRY	(abruptly) Would you kindly not interfere when I'm carrying out my official function. (He gives her a withering look.) Now, sir. I take it you realise that you are contravening the Road Traffic Act 1965 by parking your vehicle in a restricted zone?
TRAVERS	I'm here on official business.
HARRY	I'm afraid that won't do, sir. Your name?
TRAVERS	Inspector Travers, C.I.D.
ETHEL	Oh, good Lord!
RUBY	A policeman!
HARRY	(writing) Inspector Travis, C.I.D.
TRAVERS	(writing) And your name I believe is Harold Lovelock?

HARRY   Never mind that. Address?

TRAVERS   City Police Station, Conduit Street.

HARRY   (writing)   - Station, Conduit Street.

TRAVERS   (writing)   And yours is 110, Frampton Road.

HARRY   Are you trying to take the mickey out of me?

ETHEL   Tell him, Inspector, please. Don't let him drivel on making a fool of himself.

HARRY   Now watch it, Ethel!

TRAVERS   (holding up the five pound note)   Do you see what I'm holding in my hand, Mr Lovelock?

HARRY   That's not going to help you, sir.

TRAVERS   It's a five pound note.

HARRY   I know. I ought to - I've been spending 'em hand over fist these past couple of days.

ETHEL   He knows.

TRAVERS   This is one of them - spent at Randall's Furnishings last Tuesday and part of fifteen hundred pounds stolen from Cottrel's Bank in April.

HARRY   Stolen?   (To ETHEL.)   Did he say stolen?

               (ETHEL nods.)

               (to TRAVERS)   I hope you don't think I -

ETHEL   Oh, Harry! What've you done?

HARRY   What do you mean what have I done? I haven't done anything.   (To TRAVERS.)   There must be some mistake.

TRAVERS   There's no mistake.

GRAN   He ought to be locked up.

HARRY   You keep out of it!   (Panicking. To ETHEL.) Don't just stand there, Ethel - say something. Tell him I didn't do it. Go on, tell him. Tell him I found it. (To TRAVERS.)   I found it.   (Appealing to RUBY.) You say something to him, Ruby.

TRAVERS   I must warn you, Mr Lovelock, that you're not obliged to say anything, but anything you do say will be taken down and used in evidence.

HARRY   I'll tell you what I'll do. I'll forget I ever saw your car parked out there if you'll forget –

(TRAVERS stands shaking his head.)

(shaking his head)   I found it.

TRAVERS   I see, perhaps you wouldn't mind telling me where you found it?

HARRY   You really want to know?

TRAVERS   I do.

HARRY   You're never going to believe this in a thousand years.

TRAVERS   Try me.

HARRY   Stuck up an owl's – stuffed in an owl.

TRAVERS   I see. Stuffed in an owl? I must say it's original.

HARRY   (desperately)   It's the truth. You must believe me.

TRAVERS   You're quite sure it wasn't a magpie? I understand they can be real little kleptomaniacs.

HARRY   No, it was an owl. They'll tell you.   (To the others.) It was an owl, wasn't it?   (To TRAVERS.)   Its eyes lit up.   (To the others.)   Tell him how the eyes lit up.

(They all remain silent.)

What's the matter with you? Has the cat got your tongues? Did I or did I not find it stuffed in an owl?

ETHEL   (apologetically)   I don't know, Harry. We weren't in the room.

HARRY   (losing control of himself)   I know you weren't in the room. But I showed it to you when you came down.

TRAVERS   It's no good losing your temper, sir.

HARRY   How would you like it if they were on your side? They're my witnesses.

TRAVERS	Have you still got the bird?
HARRY	(suddenly dawning on him) That's it! Of course! Why didn't I think of that? If you see the bird you'll know I'm telling the truth. (He quickly moves up to wall cupboard, opens the door and takes down the owl which has now been restuffed and looks as good as new. Proudly he hands it to TRAVERS.)
TRAVERS	(examining the owl) This is it, is it?
HARRY	Yes.
TRAVERS	(squeezing it) You're quite sure?
HARRY	Of course I'm sure.
TRAVERS	Then perhaps you wouldn't mind explaining why it's still so plump if it had all that money inside it?
HARRY	I had him refilled. I made him a promise before I cut him open that I'd –
TRAVERS	I think you'd better come down to the station with me, Mr Lovelock.
HARRY	Why, are you going away?
TRAVERS	No, but I've got a feeling you might be – for quite some time.
ETHEL	Oh, no!
HARRY	I can explain –
TRAVERS	Down at the station. Here, (He gives HARRY the owl.) you can take that with you for company if you like.
	(HARRY stands holding the owl. The eyes start to flash on and off.)
	Let's be going, sir.
ETHEL	(bursting into tears) Oh, Harry!
RUBY	(bursting into tears) Oh, dad!
GRAN	Make sure he doesn't try to escape.
	(TRAVERS takes HARRY by the arm and leads him out..

ETHEL and RUBY sob copiously.)

RUBY   (between sobs)   Who's going to give me away?

GRAN   Nobody, luv. If we all keep our mouths shut they can lock him up for twenty years and no one need be any the wiser.   (She starts to open a fresh packet of ginger biscuits.)

(HARRY appears in the doorway.)

HARRY   (to GERALD)   Have you still got that form I gave you?

(GERALD at first looks puzzled, then nods.)

Well, where it says 'occupation of guarantor' you'd better write in 'gaol bird'.

(There is a fresh wail from ETHEL and RUBY. TRAVERS appears, takes HARRY by the arm and drags him off.)

ETHEL   Don't take him away, please!

(ETHEL goes out, followed by RUBY dragging GERALD. GRAN is left alone on the stage.)

GRAN   (muttering to herself)   Now perhaps we shall have a bit of peace and quiet.   (She is about to dunk a ginger nut in her mug when the handle comes away in her hand, spilling the tea in her lap. Leaping up, outraged.) He planned that! The wretch!   (Shouting after him.) Just you wait until they let you out! Just you wait!

CURTAIN

Scene 2

The following week. Eve of the wedding about 11 p.m.

When the curtain rises we see that all the new furniture has gone, along with the curtains, carpet and television. An old blanket is pinned up at the window. The dining table has been replaced by the kitchen table and is surrounded by three kitchen chairs and a packing case.

The three women are on stage wearing their dressing gowns,
ready for bed. ETHEL sits at the table with a quarter filled
bottle of port in front of her. RUBY sits at the table, and
GRAN in her own chair. They each have a small glass and
look thoroughly fed-up. There is a long pause.

ETHEL   If he knows what's good for him he won't come home.
           (Pause.)   I thought we'd have a few drinks and an
           early night. 'I won't be long', he said. That was at six
           thirty. Look at it now - gone eleven.

GRAN   You should've stopped him.

ETHEL   How could I? He said he was going to the Police Station
           to collect the reward.

GRAN   He'll've had it spent by now.

ETHEL   He'd better not. We need that to buy our old furniture
           back.   (She looks round the room and starts to sniff.)
           I'll never get over the humiliation of all that lovely new
           furniture being carted in one day and out again the next.
           The worst part was they used the same van drivers. They
           kept giving me a very peculiar look, as if I was mental.

GRAN   There's only one mental case in this house.

ETHEL   I dread to think what the neighbours are saying.

RUBY   They haven't got over the day dad was taken away in the
           police car. They're convinced he's one of the Train Gang.

ETHEL   He hates trains.

RUBY   You wouldn't think so to hear them talk.   (Suddenly
           bursting into tears.)   I'm getting married under a
           cloud.

ETHEL   (comforting her)   Now, now, luv, it's not as bad as
           that.

RUBY   It's not how I imagined it would be at all. I thought I'd
           be feeling excited and happy.

ETHEL   It's nerves.

RUBY   It's not. It's not knowing where we're going to sleep
           tomorrow night.

ETHEL   . That's all been settled. You and Gerald are having our room, so don't worry. Mrs Forbes is lending us a bed until we get ours back.

GRAN   Is there any more port left?

ETHEL   Don't you think you've had enough? This was a freshly opened bottle tonight and Ruby and me've only had a glass apiece.   (She holds up the bottle.)

GRAN   (sulking)   Are you saving that for the christening?

ETHEL   You can have some more if you really want some.

GRAN   I think I prefer port wine and ginger nuts to tea and ginger nuts.

ETHEL   Don't get hooked, because after tomorrow you're back on tea.   (Crossing to RUBY.)   How about you, luv?

(RUBY shakes her head.)

No, I don't think I will either. I want to keep a clear head in case your dad turns up. I must say I'm surprised Gerald hasn't popped in to wish you luck for tomorrow.

RUBY   He can't. He's having a stag party.

ETHEL   What stags does he know?

RUBY   He didn't say. He was very reluctant to talk about it.

GRAN   They always are. You want to stamp that out from tomorrow onwards. Where he goes you go.

ETHEL   It's only to be hoped your stag doesn't drink too much. If he's anything like he was after last years New Year's Eve party the vicar won't know whether to marry him or bury him.

RUBY   He promised he'd be careful.

ETHEL   I hope he is for your sake. There's nothing worse than a man taking vows under the influence. He uses it as an excuse for the rest of his married life.   (Mocking.) 'I'd've never said that if I'd been sober' - they're clever. (She looks at the clock.)   I wonder where Harry's got to? You don't think the police might've kept him again, do you?

GRAN   It'd be too much to hope for.

ETHEL   They wouldn't. They've got no reason. He proved that he
            never stole the money. Besides they've got it all back
            except the five shillings for your mug and he gave them
            that out of his own pocket.

GRAN   If we're going to sit up all night waiting for him, can we
            have a bit more coal on the fire?

ETHEL   There's no need for you to stay up. Why don't you go up
            to bed?

GRAN   I don't want to miss the excitement of his homecoming.

ETHEL   (crossing to the fire)   There's going to be no excite-
            ment. I'm just going to kill him that's all.   (She puts
            a couple of lumps of coal on the fire and tidies the hearth.
            She finds a piece of screwed up paper and is about to
            throw it on the fire but changes her mind and opens it out.)

GRAN   What've you found?

ETHEL   I don't know.   (Glancing at it.)   Oh, it's just an
            old letter of Harry's.   (She is about to screw it up
            again, then stops.)   That's odd - it's written on Folk
            Festival Club paper.

GRAN   What does it say?

ETHEL   I've never stooped so low as to go round reading his
            private correspondence.

GRAN   Then let me.

ETHEL   Certainly not.   (Pause.)   I don't suppose there's
            any harm in me glancing at it.

GRAN   If you're going to glance at it you might as well glance at
            it out loud.

ETHEL   (giving in)   Oh, all right, I shouldn't think for a
            minute it'll be anything important.   (Reading from the
            letter.)   'Dear Harry. I don't suppose you of all
            people need reminding that it's the Club's twentieth
            anniversary on Wednesday the twenty third, but your
            friends and fellow members have suggested I drop you this
            note to make sure that you will be there for this auspicious

occasion. Yours sincerely, Oliver Burke'.

RUBY   Today's the twenty third.

ETHEL   I know – and he'll have missed it.   (She screws up the
            letter and throws it into the grate.)   And he'll miss all
            the other anniversaries, not to mention the weekly
            practices and those embarrassing displays in the park on
            summer evenings. It's a part of your dad's life which is
            behind him, gone and forgotten for ever.

GRAN   Just like his birds.

ETHEL   (smugly)   As you say, mother, just like his birds.

            (Suddenly there is a cacophany of sound offstage. A fife
            and drum can just be distinguished above the sound of
            drunken revelry, playing 'The Floral Dance'. The three
            women look startled.)

            What in thunder is that?

            (ETHEL opens the door and at that moment four men enter,
            three dressed in the costumes of Morris dancers. The fourth,
            GERALD, wears an old mac and a flat cap but has bells
            round his knees and arms. GERALD and two of the other
            men are astride hobby horses, while the other plays a fife
            and drum. (Music over gram.) They are all drunk and
            noisy. Even so they execute an authentic traditional
            country dance.)

            (angrily)   What's the meaning of this?

            (The men continue to dance ignoring her. During the
            course of the dance GERALD comes face to face with
            RUBY.)

RUBY   (shocked)   Gerald!

ETHEL   Not Gerald, surely?   (While trying to stop them she
            gets involved in the dance.)   Stop it! Stop it! Stop
            it at once, do you hear me!

GRAN   (who has climbed on to her chair. Shouts)   Get the
            brutes out, Ethel!

ETHEL   (turning to GRAN)   What do you think I'm trying to do?

            (One of the dancers noses his horse into her back. She

swings herself round and slaps his face.)

Get your horse off me!   (Threatening them.)   If
you're not out of this house in two minutes, I'll call the
police.   (She crosses to GRAN.)   This is Harry's
doing. It's got his stamp all over it.   (Shouting at the
top of her voice.)   It's no good you hiding, Harry.
You've got it to come wherever you are!

(HARRY appears in the doorway dressed in his Morris
costume with his arm round a huge ostrich. He is very
drunk and very happy. He staggers into the room with the
aid of the bird.)

Oh, no!

(HARRY pats the bird, lets go of its neck and unsteadily
joins in the remainder of the dance. When the music stops
GERALD collapses with his horse below the table. RUBY
rushes to him and nurses his head in her lap.)

(to the men)   Now, get out, all of you, get out.

(They all start to stagger towards the door, including
HARRY.)

(pulling HARRY back into the room)   That doesn't
include you.

(As the others are hustled out by ETHEL they call out
'Goodnight, Harry!'.)

(glaring back at HARRY)   A good night is one thing
he won't be having. Go on, out you go.   (She
follows them off.

(HARRY staggers across to his ostrich and moves with it to
GRAN.)

GRAN   (cringing in her chair)   Don't come near me!

HARRY   He won't hurt you.   (To ostrich.)   You won't hurt
her, will you?

GRAN   You drunken monster!

HARRY   (to ostrich)   I said she'd say that, didn't I? He's had
four Guinnesses.   (He staggers.)

GRAN   Ugh! Disgusting!

HARRY   It is disgusting. I hate a bird what can't hold its liquor.
              (To bird.)   Stand still you bloomin' thing!

              (ETHEL comes into the room in high dudgeon, slams the
              door and stands glaring at HARRY.)

              Hello, luv, have you been out? Have - have you met - ?
              (He indicates the bird.)   You're very quiet. Anything
              the matter? There's something wrong. I can tell. Do you
              want to have a little tête-à-tête with me?

ETHEL   I never want to have anything to do with you again. Look
              at you - you're a disgrace to the human race.

HARRY   Am I? I wonder what they're going to say about him when
              (Patting the ostrich.)   he gets back to the National
              Wildfowl Trust?   (Confidentially.)   I wouldn't
              like to have his head in the morning. I know now why
              they bury them in the sand.

ETHEL   Shut up!

HARRY   Yes, luv.

RUBY   (anxiously)   Mam, mam, come and have a look at
              Gerald - I think he's dead.

HARRY   Don't blame me for that. I never laid a finger on him.

              (ETHEL crosses to RUBY and examines GERALD.)

ETHEL   He's not dead, luv. I bet he wishes he was when he comes
              round. He's drunk - like that other article over there.

HARRY   He should never have ought to had that second sip. He
              was half seas over after the first.

RUBY   You had no right to encourage him.

HARRY   (annoyed)   Now, just a minute, young lady -
              (He moves a couple of uncertain steps towards RUBY only
              to quickly return to the support of the ostrich.)   Now,
              just a minute, young lady. I didn't invite him. He just
              happened.

ETHEL   Keep quiet.

HARRY   Yes, luv. Just so long as we keep the records straight. I didn't –

ETHEL   You've caused enough trouble these last few days to last a lifetime. And now to cap it all you have to come home like this and with him   (Pointing to GERALD.) like that. Look at him. Go on, take a good look at him. Heaven only knows what sort of condition he's going to be in for the service tomorrow. We'll be lucky if we can get him right for his honeymoon.

RUBY   Oh, mam, don't say that!

ETHEL   You've got to face facts, luv, he's not very well. (To HARRY.)   I don't suppose there is any need for me to tell you this is the end? After the wedding tomorrow you'll not only be losing a daughter but the whole family.

HARRY   Now, look, Ethel –

ETHEL   I won't look any more, Harry. You've chosen to go your own sweet way. Fair enough. Go to your club, drink yourself sick, bring home your birds –

HARRY   I can explain about Horace here – the lads at the club presented me with it – I –

ETHEL   Then I hope you'll both be very happy together. I've had enough.

HARRY   (getting worked up)   You've had enough! You've had enough! What about me, eh? What about me?

ETHEL   You've had too much.

HARRY   It's nothing but nag, nag, nag. I can't do anything right. I don't know why you married me.

GRAN   Neither do I.

HARRY   (looking round)   Who said that?

GRAN   I did.

HARRY   Madam Shylock! I was wondering when you'd come for your pound of flesh. I've only got one thing to say to you – and that's belt up!

GRAN   (protesting)   Ethel!

ETHEL   That's right. Take it out on a defenceless old lady.

HARRY	Her defenceless? Don't make me laugh. There are more spines on her than a bloody porcupine.
ETHEL	I think you'd better go up to your room, mother.
HARRY	No, let her stay. It's about time she heard the truth about herself. (To GRAN.) You're a nasty, spiteful, old lady. You've done nothing but come between me and Ethel ever since we've been married.
GRAN	How dare you?
HARRY	I'll tell you how I dare - because I'm full of beer. I don't care. I shall care in the morning, but I don't care now. I've kept quiet for twenty five years and that's long enough.
GRAN	I warned you, Ethel. I warned you this would happen.
HARRY	You and your warnings! Every three months you predict we're going to blow ourselves up, but we're still here, aren't we?
GRAN	The day will come.
HARRY	Well when it does I only hope the devil has a good supply of ginger nuts or there'll be no living with you.
ETHEL	(outraged) Harry!
HARRY	When we got married you knew what I was. You knew I had hobbies and you were all for them.
ETHEL	You were younger then.
HARRY	I can't help growing old. I've been taking Phyllosan since I was thirty five but it's been a losing battle. You used to be proud of me. When other wives boasted about their husbands you used to say, 'I've got one at home just like him - with bells on'. (He shakes a leg and the bells ring.)
	(ETHEL smiles.)
	It used to be our little joke.
ETHEL	That was a long time ago.
HARRY	I know.
ETHEL	There's no point in raking up the past. It's all over now.

Come on, mother, Ruby, it's time we were in bed.

RUBY   But mam, what are we going to do about Gerald?

ETHEL   That's your dad's problem - he brought him here, let him
                get him home.

HARRY   Oh, no you don't! I'm not carrying him through the
                streets.

ETHEL   Then give him a lift on your friend   (She points to the
                ostrich.)   only get him out.

RUBY   (staring down at GERALD)   Goodnight, sweetheart -

HARRY   (bursting into song)   - 'See you in the morning - '

                (RUBY gives GERALD a kiss on the forehead.)

RUBY   (to ETHEL)   I hope he's feeling better in the morning.

ETHEL   I'll be satisfied if he has feelings in the morning.

                (GRAN and RUBY go out. ETHEL is about to follow them
                off.)

HARRY   Ethel.

ETHEL   (turning)   What?

HARRY   About tomorrow. You don't have to leave. I'll go - I'll
                find somewhere and -

ETHEL   We'll discuss it in the morning when you're sober.

HARRY   How about when I come up to bed?

ETHEL   You're not coming up to bed tonight. I'll put you a
                pillow and a couple of blankets in the bath. You can
                make do in there.

HARRY   (protesting)   The taps leak.

ETHEL   Only the cold.

HARRY   Oh, hell!

ETHEL   I'm away then.   (She turns to leave.)

HARRY   Just a minute. I suppose it's no good to say I'm sorry?

ETHEL   Not now.

HARRY   Because I am.

ETHEL   It's the beer talking.

HARRY   (looking up at the ostrich)   We both are.

ETHEL   That's what I mean. It's too late, Harry, to be sorry.

HARRY   Maybe you're right. I just thought I'd mention it.

ETHEL   If only I could be sure you really meant it.

HARRY   I do. Honest.

ETHEL   I'd like to give you another chance.

HARRY   (eagerly)   Then why don't you? Why don't we try
               and make a fresh start? I don't mean like other times. I
               mean a real fresh start. I'll tell you what. How about a
               second honeymoon?

ETHEL   At our age?

HARRY   I don't see why not. If I double up on me Phyllosan I
               might be able to pull off a few surprises.

ETHEL   (a little bashful)   Don't be silly. Anyway, it's out of
               the question.

HARRY   I don't see why.

ETHEL   What about mother?

HARRY   We can put her in a kennels, send her out with meals on
               wheels - we could sort out something.

ETHEL   I must say it would be nice to get away for a bit.

HARRY   Just the two of us. Even to say it sounds nice. I've got
               the reward money here somewhere.   (He starts to
               search for it. The search grows more and more frantic.)

ETHEL   You haven't gone and lost it have you?

HARRY   No, no, it's here.   (Anxiously.)   I had it.
               (He finds it tucked down one trouser leg. He pulls the
               trouser out of the top of his stocking and the money drops
               out.)

               (To ETHEL.)   I could read your thoughts then.
               (Holding up the bundle of notes.)   There's three

hundred and fifty quid here. Enough to buy a bit of new
furniture with a bit left over for a spree. What do you say?

ETHEL   I'll have to think about it.

HARRY   You do that.

GRAN   (voice off)   Are you all right down there, Ethel? Is
            he trying anything on?

HARRY   (shouting back angrily)   No I'm not, you old bat!

ETHEL   (shouting up)   I'm just coming, mother.   (To
            HARRY.)   You shouldn't antagonise her.

HARRY   She starts it –

ETHEL   I know she can be difficult at times, but you must
            remember her age.

HARRY   I do. That's why I don't hit her.

ETHEL   I'm going up now, Harry, and when I come down in the
            morning I don't want to see that there   (She points to
            the ostrich.)   and I want to see him   (Pointing to
            GERALD.)   in church, on time, looking ready,
            willing and able. Do I make myself clear?

HARRY   Yes, luv.

ETHEL   Just make sure that there are no complications, Harry,
            because if there are I won't be held responsible for my
            actions.

HARRY   No, luv.

ETHEL   Goodnight then.

HARRY   Goodnight, luv.

            (ETHEL turns to go out.)

            By the way, are we friends again?

ETHEL   (giving him a warm smile)   I suppose so.

HARRY   In that case there's no need for me to sleep in the bath, is
            there?

            (ETHEL gives him a kiss on the cheek.)

            How about one for Horace?   (He laughs.)

(ETHEL goes out. HARRY stands motionless for a second or so with his arm round the neck of the ostrich.)

HARRY (turning and looking at GERALD)   Come on, Gerald lad, let's go.

(GERALD does not stir.)

I said let's go.   (To the ostrich.)   Excuse me. (He lets go of it and attempts to cross to GERALD until he realises he is not going to make it unaided. He moves back for the bird.)   You'll have to come with me. (He puts his arm about its neck and wheels it towards GERALD. As he does so there is a noisy rattle from inside the ostrich. He stops and looks at the bird.)   Was that you or me?   (He rattles his bells.)   It wasn't me.   (He takes the bird by the neck and shakes it violently.)   It was you! Do you want to tinkle? (He shakes it again.)   I don't like the sound of that. I think they've been feeding you the wrong kind of birdseed. Don't worry. I've got just the thing to bring express relief. Wait there.   (He staggers up to tea-chest and returns with the bread knife.)   Kildare strikes again!   (He approaches the bird from the rear, thrusts the knife on to the zip fastener running the full length of the underside of the bird and makes to cut. Out tumbles a couple of crowns, a sceptre, an orb, a heavy gold chain, golden goblets, all looking very much as if they might be the Crown Jewels. He looks at them in amazement. Nervously he picks up one of the crowns, stands staring at it then hangs it on the ostrich's head. Quickly he picks up the orb and sceptre and stands holding the orb in his left hand and the sceptre in his right. He stands not knowing what to do for the best.)   Oh, hell!   (He calls weakly.)   Ethel! Ethel! I think we've got a slight complication!

CURTAIN

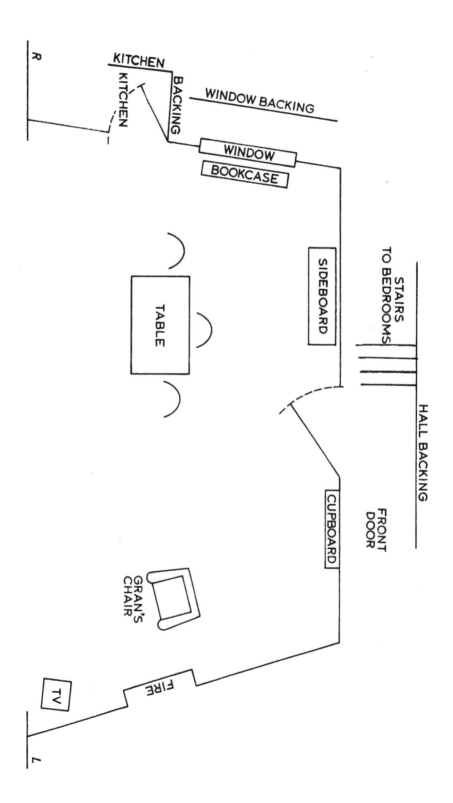

PROPERTY PLOT

ACT I Scene 1

Cases of stuffed birds (Set)
Biscuit tin)
Teapot)
Milk jug) set on table
Sugar basin)
Cup and saucer (ETHEL)
Mug (GRAN)
Ginger biscuits (GRAN)
List (RUBY)
Paper bag (GERALD)
Loose ginger biscuits (GERALD)
Handkerchief (GERALD)
Inhaler (GERALD)
Picture (set over fireplace)
Aerosol spray (set in sideboard)
Ticket book (HARRY)
Pencil (HARRY)

ACT I Scene 2

Tray with cutlery, etc. (ETHEL)
Stuffed owl (HARRY)
Haversack (HARRY)
Packet ginger biscuits (HARRY)
Plate of pilchards (ETHEL)
Ticket book in haversack
(HARRY)
Newspaper (Set)
Cherub and bowl wrapped in
sacking (Set)
Parking ticket (GERALD)
Handkerchief (RUBY)
Five pound notes (in owl)
Bread knife (set in sideboard)
Handkerchief (HARRY)
Bag of copper (in owl)
3 suitcases (ETHEL, RUBY, GRAN)

Knives (set in sideboard)
Feathers (set offstage)

ACT II Scene 1

Rubber plant (ETHEL)
New mug (GRAN)
Six packets ginger biscuits (set
by GRAN's chair)
Dressbox with wedding dress, etc.
(set offstage)
Pound notes (HARRY)
Bill in dressbox
Large brown paper parcel
(GERALD)
Peg bag with pegs (set offstage)
Newspaper (set)
Five pound note (TRAVERS)
Official form (HARRY)
Black notebook (TRAVERS)
Black notebook (HARRY)
Pencil (TRAVERS)
Pencil (HARRY)
Owl (set in cupboard)

ACT II Scene 2

Bottle of port (set on table)
3 glasses (RUBY, GRAN, ETHEL)
Piece of screwed up paper (set
in hearth)
Coal (set)
Hobby horses (set offstage)
Ostrich (set offstage. HARRY)
Bundle of paper money (HARRY)
Bread knife (set in tea chest)
Crown Jewels (in ostrich)

PRODUCTION NOTE

In presenting this play pace is the essence, not rush. Cues should be picked up quickly so as not to allow the production to drop.

While the entire movement of the piece is based on the continuous bickering between Harry, Ethel and Gran, any spite which exists must be coated with a heavy layer of humour, which the script provides but which must also come from the artists involved. The bitterness is fleeting and the needling always fun. The producer should remember one thing above all else while he or she is directing - that however far fetched the situations, however large the characters, it is still basically a play about a family, not a circus filled with clowns.

The set is quite simple, as you will see from the ground plan and should present few problems. The props are everyday, apart from the ostrich which can easily be constructed from wood and wire netting covered in canvas. If anyone has any ostrich feathers then these used for wings and tail feathers will help the overall effect. The owl, which is plastic, can be bought for a few shillings from a shop which sells garden ornaments. It should stand about a foot high. Feathers can be stuck all over it to make it more realistic. The eyes are removed and small torch bulbs inserted in their place, connected to a flat battery.

CHARACTERS

ETHEL   is a typical working class housewife, disillusioned, short of money and short on temper. Having mother living with her ever since she was married has, without doubt, affected her relationship with Harry. Ethel over the years has become an Othello to her mother's Iago.

MRS CARD (GRAN)   has her hand firmly on the spoon and derives enormous satisfaction from stirring up trouble between Harry and the rest of the family. It is important that the audience enjoy not liking her as a character but they must never be allowed to dislike the actress playing the part.

RUBY   is an attractive girl of nineteen. She is sensible, for the most part bright and cheerful. What she sees in her fiancé, Gerald, is hard to understand. They do say opposites attract so perhaps it is best to leave it at that.

HARRY   sins as much as he is sinned against. His is a rich, noisy, steamroller performance. He runs the full gamut of comic emotions, from aggression to self-pity. It is essential that he antagonises Ethel and Gran, but not the audience.

GERALD   They certainly don't come any more odd than Gerald. His is possibly the most difficult part in the play. He must not be clowned, though the temptation to do so is great. The best way to approach the part is for the actor to think like a red nose comic during the early rehearsals and tone down until he achieves the balance of a comic performance and the very real misery of a slow-witted young man suffering permanently from a head cold. It is a part which has to be felt to be realised.

MR TRAVERS   is a policeman. He is without a sense of humour. He should be played straight within the context of the play and not be caricatured in any way.

MADE AND PRINTED IN GREAT BRITAIN BY
LATIMER TREND & COMPANY LTD PLYMOUTH

MADE IN ENGLAND